MOTHERS AND DAUGHTERS

Searching for
New
Connections

MOTHERS
AND
DAUGHTERS

Ann F. Caron, Ed.D.

Henry Holt and Company
New York

Henry Holt and Company, Inc.
Publishers since 1866
115 West 18th Street
New York, New York 10011

Henry Holt® is a registered
trademark of Henry Holt and Company, Inc.

Library of Congress Cataloging-in-Publication Data
Caron, Ann F.
Mothers and daughters : searching for new connections / Ann F. Caron.
p.   cm.
Includes index.
ISBN 0-8050-5149-X (alk. paper)
1. Mothers and daughters—United States.   2. Young women—
United States—Psychology.   I. Title.
HQ755.86.C37   1998
306.874'3—dc21   97-52977

First Edition 1998

Designed by Kate Nichols

Printed in the United States of America
All first editions are printed on acid-free paper. ∞

10   9   8   7   6   5   4   3   2   1

To my mother,

Mildred Collins Fitzgerald,

with love and gratitude

Contents

Acknowledgments

I am deeply grateful to the young women and the mothers who showed me the importance of connections. The young women who invited me into their homes, gathered friends, and opened their hearts to me have my profound thanks. From across the country, these women inspired and challenged me. My hope was to accurately capture their feelings, their dreams, their ambitions. I thank them for allowing me to portray their generation.

I also am indebted to mothers, women in midlife, who welcomed me and talked openly about their daughters and their lives. We, as mothers of daughters, shared many of the milestones of the past and concerns about the future. Their words made the writing of this book a much easier task. Thank you.

The research about women's development has expanded dramatically during the decade I have been writing about women and their daughters. However, the work generated by the Wellesley College Centers for Women (the merger of the Center for Research on Women and the Stone Center) has been particularly helpful. Their research forms the theoretical basis of this book.

Thanks to Meredith Welch, a friend, my first reader, and mother of a 25-year-old daughter, who told me when she thought I was on target and questioned me when she thought I wasn't. I am grateful for her help.

My thanks always to Molly Friedrich, my literary agent, and Cynthia Vartan, my editor, who encouraged me to pursue these ideas and allowed me the freedom to develop them. They have been my team through three books, and I rely heavily on their good judgment.

My husband, John, constantly assured me that everything could be put on hold until after the deadline. His love sustains me always. Thank you, John.

Our daughters-in-law, Dede, Jane, Andrea, and Lisa, offered stories and good advice which are embedded in these pages. Our sons, their husbands, John, Peter, Paul, and Mark, thought it was great that I was writing about women this time. Thank you all for your love and solicitude.

Thanks to our daughter Elizabeth, who first made me aware of the quandary of young women seeking careers. She and her husband, Abdellatif, offered warm meals and good company during this project. Thank you both.

Cathleen, our youngest daughter, represents beautifully this generation of young women. She inspired me to write this book and was always just a phone call away. Thank you, Cathleen.

Finally, my mother, Mildred Collins Fitzgerald, has made my life and the lives of our children fuller and richer. It is to her this book is lovingly dedicated.

MOTHERS AND DAUGHTERS

Introduction

When I told my 26-year-old daughter that I was going to research and write about two generations, young women and their mothers, she laughed. Recalling that I had written about adolescent girls when she was a senior in high school, she asked, "Are you always going to write about me and my friends?" Then she paused and added, "You'll have a lot to write about."

My daughter was right. As I interviewed young women, I was continually impressed with their awareness of being a unique generation. Although they are grateful for their many opportunities, they often feel overburdened and anxious. They realize that they are the first generation of women to grow up knowing that every door would open to them. They did not have to integrate their schools by gender or race. They do not have to endure the discomfort of being the token woman at work. They do not feel the same pressure to marry that their mothers felt.

However, they also are the first generation to feel the effects of widespread divorce. (In the midseventies, divorce surpassed death as the leading cause of the dissolution of marriage.) Aware that vows made are easily broken, young women have become wary. They are inclined to postpone marriage until they have established security for themselves.

They also realize that the promiscuity that enticed them in high school has left in its wake unfulfilled relationships—as well as AIDS and more prevalent sexually transmitted diseases. Not willing to risk their emotional or physical health, they have become more cautious about their partners.

More than fear motivates them. These young women feel a strong sense of responsibility. "At some point, you have to take responsibility for yourself and not blame your parents or someone else," a 25-year-old acknowledged. They value themselves and others. They are reliable, trustworthy, work hard, and they expect their efforts to be appreciated.

But the first years out of college are difficult. The wide range of options often leaves them in a state of "option paralysis." They know a lot is expected of them because they have been assured that they can accomplish anything. Knowing what to do, however, is not easy. Not until they reach their midtwenties do they become more confident and sure of their choices.

I love their forthrightness, their ability to talk about their dilemmas with honesty, their lack of pretense, their humor, their friendliness, and their ambition. In my interviews, I was particularly moved by the affection young women expressed for their mothers (who were not present during their interviews). They actually like their mothers and try their best to understand them.

This new attitude toward mothers presents a sharp contrast to a teenage daughter's reluctance to understand her mother at all, especially her reasons for setting limits. Now young women talk about how grateful they are that their mothers rescued them from disaster during adolescence. When I heard this, I wanted to call a press conference and assure mothers that the anxiety-producing days of adolescence were over. Their struggle to keep loving their daughters was well worth it.

Young women do not want to *be* their mothers, however.

Most will not marry, as I did, at age 23 and begin a family. They want to develop themselves first and establish their own paths. They have the ability and the desire, but the way is untrod. They do not want to give up either family or career possibilities. They are setting new standards for themselves and constantly question their motives, their goals, the reality of their expectations.

Mothers of young women also are searching for new connections, new ways of expressing themselves in midlife. Their voices reflect their experience, their satisfaction, their restlessness. No longer faced with the same type of family responsibilities, they are looking for recognition of themselves. They want to be accepted for who they are, not for their job, not for their husband, not for their children. This, they feel, is their time, their time to reconnect with old ambitions or form new ones. They search for connections to friends, to different work environments, to spiritual depths. Their voices at times reflect their daughters' "What am I going to do?"

This book is about the differences and similarities between these two generations of women. Mothers and daughters speak freely and clearly about their joys, frustrations, disappointments, hopes, dreams. One message stands above all others. In both stages of life, they are searching for connections. Their connections to each other may form the underpinning of that search, but they reach beyond that mutual bond. They search also for connections to other people.

I hope the voices in this book will help mothers and daughters truly understand and appreciate each other. The names and the places are not real, but their voices are. Their generational influences differ, their manner of speaking differs, their goals differ, but their dreams of finding themselves through connections are the same.

1

The Transition to Adulthood: The College Years

A "Transition into Equality"

When Denise, age 52, asked her daughter, Jill, a junior in college, to describe the ideal college mother, Jill responded that such a mother is able to make a "transition into equality." She hoped that she and her mother would develop an equal "give-and-take."

Jill envisions an enviable adult mother-daughter relationship—a sharing between equals. But a "transition into equality" comes slowly between a mother and daughter, who have just emerged from the adolescent years of "give and take" criticism, not encouragement. During adolescence, a mother tries to mold her daughter into a perfect woman, or at least an acceptable woman, while at the same time her daughter is struggling to establish her uniqueness, her own self. The often acrimonious, and sometimes hilariously absurd, exchanges that arise between mother and daughter begin during middle school and may last well into high school.

But now the daughter has graduated from high school; her adolescence is over. The mother breathes a sigh of relief because her daughter has emerged from the emotional turbulence of imbalanced hormones and fifteen-minute mood swings. Her body and mind are in sync, and she is safe. But just as mother and daughter once again begin to appreciate each other, the daughter leaves for college.

Over eight million women now attend college, composing 55.1 percent of the total enrollment. In 1966, when many of their mothers were college-age, only two and one-half million women attended college.[1] This change in women's educational opportunities requires another shift in the relationship between mother and daughter. Just as a daughter must adjust to her new status as a college woman, not a high-school girl, her mother must adapt to her daughter's adulthood.

Preparing for Freshman Year

Sometimes the social scene during the summer before college delays the new, more peaceful, accommodation between mother and daughter. It can be grueling for families as a daughter often begins acting like a freshman, ignoring parental restrictions, and almost guaranteeing that her family will be happy to see her leave. This blip in the new harmony between mother and daughter occurs because the daughter fears leaving home, family, and friends. Her insecurity surfaces as she faces the prospect of living with unfamiliar roommates, coed dormitories and bathrooms, and an unrestrained social life. She may not feel prepared for this freedom—and for good reason.

Not everyone fits easily into a college campus. A mother and father who are sensitive to their daughter's needs can assure her that she has the ability to make good choices, that they trust her and are confident she will make the right decisions. However, she still may cover up her nervousness and want to spend all her time with friends, accumulating memories of their last summer together. The summer before college should be a time of reassurances and love from her family, not a summer of constant arguing.

Abbie's daughter Trina wanted to go to a college as far away as possible, and she fought with Abbie about her college choice, her curfews, and her boyfriend all that summer. "It was a mother-daughter thing," Abbie explained. Abbie cautioned Trina that the university she chose was "too big, too far away, and too much of a party school" and urged her to change her mind while she still had other options. Trina won the argument but called home before the end of the first semester complaining that the school was "too big, too far away, and too much of a party school." Trina remained for the year, studied hard, and transferred to a smaller, closer, and more academic university—and Abbie claims that she never told Trina, "I told you so."

No matter how difficult (or easy) the summer before college is for families, fall finally arrives and the moment of departure descends. A mother must say good-bye to her daughter's childhood.

Mothers

Letting Go

I was taken by surprise by the overwhelming sadness I felt when I dropped my daughter, our youngest child, off at college. The feeling of loss that swept over me should not have surprised me since I had wept when each of our children had gone to college. But this time I thought my response would be different. With our children on their own, I would be free to pursue my own interests and a new career. Yet I wept as I walked across the campus green. I was leaving behind a part of myself, my last child, and I didn't think anything could fill the vacuum left by my children.

I resisted staying around to help my daughter unpack and arrange her room because I did not want to intrude when she was meeting roommates for the first time. Their conversations and room design had to be theirs alone. She was establishing her mark, her identity within a college dorm, and she had to do it her way. I knew that a new era was beginning for her—and for me.

However, I, like many women, wondered if life would ever be as exciting as when she and her siblings were young. I seemed to forget the fretful nights waiting to hear the garage door open to signal she was safely home. I forgot our disputes about curfews and parties and boyfriends. I could focus only on the good times we had and the fun of having a teenager in the house.

I also realized that although my relationship with her was not ended, it definitely was altered. No longer would she saunter into the kitchen and casually ask if she could visit a boyfriend away in college. Now when she wanted to go off campus, she would not have to ask anyone. No longer would I share the spontaneous joys or sorrows of the events in her life. No longer would I agonize through a late night imagining the worst scenario of smashed cars and calls from a hospital. Now her college friends would be the first to share good news and bad news, the first to hear about boyfriends, classes, and hardships. I no longer would be an intimate part of her life.

I was relieved to read that historian Doris Kearns Goodwin, age 54, felt the same way I did. She wrote in the *Time* magazine issue on baby boomers turning 50, "It wasn't so much turning 50 that had an impact [on me] as much as my youngest child's going off to school [college]. . . . The structure of your day is rounded by the kids."[2]

For some mothers more than others, the reality of daughters

depending on roommates for moral support is difficult to accept. They want to be the first to know what is happening in their daughters' lives. Cynthia, whose daughter suffered a nervous breakdown in her freshman year, did not realize the intensity of her daughter's distress until her daughter's friend called from the college infirmary to tell Cynthia that her daughter had to be hospitalized. Cynthia, upset that she did not know the magnitude of her daughter's difficulties, also realized her daughter was not alone in her despair. "I think college is very tough," Cynthia said. "Several of my daughter's friends had even a harder time than my daughter." One friend dropped out of school and spent two years in intensive therapy before she returned. Another of her classmates, an outstanding scholar and athlete, committed suicide.

Because freshman year is difficult for young women, mothers need to keep in close touch. However, every mother faces a dilemma: How much contact will be considered too much, and how much will be welcome? Will her phone calls or questions be perceived as intrusion? Now that her daughter is an adult, will advice be wanted? How much support does she need?

How Much Support?

Although parents of daughters who reside on campus are not involved with them on a day-to-day basis, studies show that parental support is essential to a student's psychological adjustment to college. After testing college freshmen, researchers found that those who received parental support were better adjusted and less distressed than were those with low parental support.[3] Maternal support was determined by asking the freshmen questions like: "Does she really understand how you feel about things?" and "Is she critical or disapproving of you?"

The second question offers a key to the success of mothers and daughters during college and perhaps for life. If a daughter suspects that her mother disapproves of her choice of classes, friends, boyfriends, she faces an even greater challenge in adjustment to college. She needs assurance from her parents that, as a young adult, she is capable of making wise decisions.

When the same researchers followed 18- to 20-year-olds into sophomore year, they found that "social support from both the mother and father and a nonconflictual relationship between parents played an important adaptive role during the transition to young adulthood."[4] The study suggests that a college student's ability to make friends easily is related to a warm attachment to her parents. A young woman who is emotionally distant from her parents, or whose parents are unhappy with each other, may find herself uncertain about how to relate to others. She may have difficulty making friends because she has not experienced what it means to be at ease with others.

Even though a daughter may have argued her way through high school, tested her mother's limits, and challenged her father's authority, she wants—and needs—their love, acceptance, and approval during college. Some students never receive that much-needed vote of confidence.

"She Wanted to Be Independent"

During her senior year in high school, Nancy really upset her parents. She challenged their religious beliefs, hung out with an "unacceptable" group of friends, wore her hair in odd ways, and accumulated earrings. She also became a first-class cyclist, entering and winning many cycling competitions. Spending more and more time alone, she stood apart from her family. When she entered college, her parents never telephoned her. She occasionally called home, and she went home for Christmas. Right before freshman parent weekend, Nancy, who was attending a traditional college, shaved off all her hair. When her parents arrived for the weekend, they brought her handsome older brother, whose appearance contrasted sharply with Nancy's unconventional style.

A week after that weekend, Nancy was killed in a biking accident. At the funeral her mother told me that Nancy had fought so hard to show that she was independent that they decided to let her go, to let her be independent. Her roommates later said that Nancy did not want to be alienated from her parents. Through long nights of talking, she told them that she wanted her parents to recognize her individuality, her uniqueness, and to realize that she was not her mother, her grandmother, or her brother. She had longed to remain connected, yet she never had the opportunity to express that longing to her parents. The distance between them had grown too great, and she did not know how to take the first step toward reconciliation. Neither did her parents.

Nancy's mother did not understand that the "rebellion" her daughter was undergoing was not a defiance of her mother but a searching for herself. If she had grasped Nancy's needs, she may have been more accepting of her lifestyle and looked at her daughter—shaved head and all—with pride, love, and even admiration. Perhaps she could have thought back to her own youth and remembered her yearnings to be someone, to do something different, her desire not to be a clone of her mother.

If Nancy and her mother had thrashed their way through their differences, their bond might not have been broken. Conflict between a mother and a daughter does not have to result in a lost relationship. Researchers from Wellesley College's Stone Center found that "conflict between late adolescent daughters [college students in their research] and their mothers is typically encapsulated around specific issues that can co-exist with the feeling that 'my mother is my best friend.' "[5]

When mothers and daughters stop talking and do not attempt to understand their differences, they create an emotional distancing that is disabling to each. If they are able to argue through their conflicts and still love each other, they keep emotionally connected. The impassioned give-and-take, the interruptions, the emotional upheavals will not harm mothers and daughters as long as they keep talking and listening to each other. "When my mother didn't talk to me for a time during college, it was the hardest time in my life," a 25-year-old woman told me as she looked back on her college days.

Not all mother-daughter pairs are volatile. Some, uncomfortable with confrontation, quietly discuss their disputes. The important point is that they remain engaged and connected. A mother's support remains critical for college-age women. Some mothers, however, overstep their boundaries, keeping their daughters dependent and inept.

"I'm Putting Her Through School"

Pam, a college freshman, flunked two classes her first semester away from home because she had never written research papers on her own. During middle school and high school, her mother not only did all her research but actually wrote her required papers. When Pam went to the opposite coast for college, she had to write her own papers for the first time since fourth grade. Needless to say, without possessing any research or writing skills, Pam could not continue in school. She returned to her hometown and enrolled in a local college where she is passing, with her mother still researching and writing her papers.

When I asked Pam's mother why she cheats for her daughter, she replied: "I'm not sorry. I think I do the right thing. I don't want her to drop out. If she has a paper to do, she doesn't do it and gets headaches when she goes to the library. The time comes closer and closer, and she begins fretting about the paper, and nothing else gets done. She doesn't pay attention in class. She can't study. She has it on her mind until I can't stand it, and I'll say, 'I'll do it.' If I do it, it's like all the pressure is off and she can relax. She can't really get mad at me cause I'm putting her through school."

Pam's mother clearly gives her daughter the wrong kind of support. Pam is under her mother's control, a pattern established in childhood, and now she cannot free herself. She depends on her mother for her survival in college. Pam would have benefited from research and writing tutoring during middle school. Now she would be better off going directly into a work environment that does not require research papers and can utilize her other skills. Perhaps at some point she could enroll in a continuing education class that teaches research and writing skills, pass the course on her own, and try college again.

Although Pam's pathological fear of writing papers is extreme, many students are challenged by academic classes. Students who obtained top grades in high school are now faced with classmates who have accomplished as much as or more than they have. Conversely, students who have fears of inadequacy may realize that their ideas/thoughts/answers are just as accomplished as their peers'. All students quickly wake up to the fact that no one is going to tell them when to study or what to study. Many mothers have received frantic phone calls right before a major paper is due and heard the cry, "I can't do it. It's too much." Rather than writing the paper for them, wise mothers realize that their daughters only want to vent their frustration about the difficulty and challenge of the workload. A good listener and a little confidence boosting are what they need, not a quick fix.

Finding the Balance

Mothers can also discover how quickly their daughters mature in college and develop the skills necessary to manage their lives. Marilyn, whose daughter, Jill, is a junior, described her daughter and her friends as "focused." "They know what they want to do, and they work for it," she said. Although many students may not manage as well as Jill, all mothers and daughters search for a more equal balance in their relationship. Mothers wonder how much support is just right.

Marilyn herself is an accomplished woman, a social worker, but acknowledges that Jill is "deeper and smarter than I am. She'll talk about something, and she knows it a lot better than I do. I've almost consciously let her move out ahead." Her daughter now recommends books for her to read and calls her about mutual interests.

In spite of her daughter's intelligence and their good relationship, Marilyn still grapples with how much support she should give her daughter. How often should she call her? How much advice should she give her? Marilyn doesn't quite feel comfortable with their being "equals"; she believes she still has to act like a mother. "There still has to be this person that she can call and fall apart to on the phone," she said. "Someone who is going to hear her out and will be more worried than anyone else will be. At the same time there is equality, there should be mother and daughter."

Marilyn and her friend discussed a common theme between mothers and daughters: how much to let go during college. "We worry about this," Marilyn said. "It's such a fine line between being readily available versus letting go a little bit. What is it that fosters a young woman being fully developed? How much do you want to be there? What's good enough, and what's too much?" They have decided that "it's better to err on the side of too much."

After my interview with Marilyn and her friend, I thought of the contrast between them and Nancy's mother. Nancy's mother did not err on the side of too much. Perhaps she never thought about how much emotional support Nancy needed because she was so angry at her for her show of independence. Her anger would not allow her to consider doing "too much."

On the other hand, Pam's mother did far too much for her daughter when she wrote her papers and made her daughter dependent on her. She undermined her daughter's ability to manage her own affairs, even though she thought she was helping her.

The question of how much support is just right can only be resolved by individual pairs of mothers and daughters. However, researchers confirm that attachment to parents during college is positively related with stability of a young person's self-esteem and life satisfaction.[6] When a daughter and mother are no longer living together year-round, telephone calls, letters, and E-mail can keep them connected. I remember listening carefully to both my daughters' voices over the phone, trying to discern any signs of sadness or unspoken disappointments. I relished in their run-down of classes and activities. They were changing, creating their own friendships, their own style and interests—an inner core that would be theirs alone.

College women appreciate a parent's vote of confidence. "My family has always instilled in me the attitude that whatever I put my mind to I can do," a college sophomore told me. "Even if there was a day when I was weak, I would think back to my family and remind myself that they believe in me. I know I can do anything. It's not a burden. There are times when I think I'm not doing well grade-wise, and I get upset. They will say 'Okay, relax. We don't expect you to be a superstar.' "

Another student appreciated her parents' sacrifices to send her to school. "My mom and dad don't have a lot, but they totally give to me and my brother and sister," she said. "My dad doesn't have a day off. He works Monday through Sunday, and it's for all of us. I think they are the most beautiful people on earth. They don't tell me you better do this or that. They just give, and they don't ask in return."

That kind of support can never be considered "too much,"

and a daughter appreciates the "transition into equality" that flows from parental support that respects her uniqueness and maturity.

Daughters

"A Time to Develop Yourself"

"I think the four years from 18 to 22 are fundamental periods of growth and personal development," a senior in a residential Midwestern college told me. "After I left high school, I was pretty confident and vain and materialistic. My value system was not fundamentally different than now, but I appreciate things in a different capacity now. I think my confidence has gained. In college you have the time to develop yourself and not worry about other things. It's a luxury a lot of people don't have."

This woman found the perfect college (for her) that gave her the time to "develop" herself before entering the world of full-time employment and independent living. But the four years (or longer for many) of college do not always pass serenely, and for some, they may be hazardous to their health.

Sex, Drugs, Eating Disorders: Social Scene 101

Gwen recalled that at her daughter's freshman orientation the dean welcomed the students and their parents, extending a special welcome to gay and lesbian freshmen. He informed the students about the drug and alcohol facilities on campus, told them where they could obtain contraceptives, and warned the women students about date rape. When the dean was finished speaking, Gwen and her husband were ready to take their daughter out of college. They had not expected the school to replicate their home life, but they were not prepared to have her encounter

such a disparate environment. Her daughter, Gwen said de-
jectedly, was offered escorts to walk around the campus at
night. They had worried about leaving their daughter, and after
the freshman orientation they were panicked. They fretted that
she was not prepared for the gritty realities of life on that campus.

The social "realities" of college often are encountered for the
first time during girls' high-school years, but the major difference
between their high school and college experiences is that their
parents are not there to set guidelines and monitor their behavior
at college. If parents discuss standards with their high-school
daughters and trust them, remaining vigilant yet trusting, their
daughters usually develop a sense of responsibility. Some college
students, however, have not developed that maturity and must
learn the hard way. When one 28-year-old reflected on her college years, she commented, "I don't know why it was so hard to
be responsible in college. I remember running to the clinic
asking, 'Where are the morning-after pills?' "

Because they are living alone or with same-age friends for
the first time, college students encounter a freedom with no
restraints. Some women find that freedom overwhelming, and
others discover their own built-in common sense.

"Parties are ridiculous," Jesse said. "People get so smashing
drunk, and I'm not having fun. I'll have a few drinks and get a
buzz, but I don't enjoy having a hangover in the morning. I did it
in freshman year. For me it was being out of the house and saying,
'I'm out. Let's go crazy.' But I've done it. I won't do it again."

Alix, now a senior, was surprised when she first arrived on
her campus. "I saw cases of alcohol stacked up on each end of
the dorm, and I was overwhelmed. I didn't expect that." She
has friends who "have to" go out every night. "I think a lot of
kids are very dependent on alcohol to have a good time. The
whole social life is going to a party and getting drunk. It's very
frustrating."

Abusive drinking by women has increased dramatically and

now is comparable to the drinking rates of men, according to the National Commission on Substance Abuse at Colleges and Universities. The commission reported that about one-third of all college women said they drank to get drunk—triple the number who reported such drinking ten years before. The report also said that about 90 percent of campus rapes, 95 percent of violent campus crime, and 80 percent of campus vandalism are alcohol related. Although some studies indicate a slight decline in campus drinking, alcohol abuse remains a major problem on college campuses.[7]

Substance-abuse prevention programs in colleges tend to focus on young males and stress drunk-driving, physical risk-taking, and vandalism. As worthy as those concerns are, one of the most dangerous connections, that of alcohol and sexual assault, is neglected in the discussions.

Alcohol and sexual assault are frequently linked in studies that examine college females. In a sample of college women from a large urban university, over half of the 1,160 women surveyed reported that they had experienced some form of sexual assault, not always from fellow students. Ninety-five percent of those assaults were committed by individuals the women knew, and almost 50 percent involved alcohol consumption by one or both parties.[8] The average age of the women at the time of the assault was 20.

No wonder parents are worried about their daughters. They realize they must send them to college with additional warnings about health and safety. But now, unlike the high-school years, they have no way of knowing what is going on in the dorms, sororities, fraternities, or off-campus housing. The in loco parentis role of the university was relinquished along with most single-sex dorms during the college revolutions of the sixties. Parents cannot rely on college administrators to oversee the social activities on a campus; they must rely solely on their daughters' use of common sense and the values they have taught them.

Those values are learned from mothers and fathers who care

and care and care some more. A daughter may complain about her mother being too strict or "on her case" too much during high school, but sometimes she misses the attention once she is out of the house. Jayne told me she now realizes what her mother was doing during her high-school years: "I understand now why she was such a pain in the neck to me. When you go away to college and you're on your own, you miss that. I probably would not admit that to her, but you know you miss someone caring all the time. I didn't hate her, but I was always telling her to leave me alone. I wanted to be with my friends."

Of course, not all sexual activity in college involves assault, but there are other dangers associated with sex in college. In a study from a southern university, 66 percent of the unmarried college students reported being sexually active during the previous three months, and one-third of that group reported having more than one sexual partner.[9] The sexually active students were putting themselves at risk for sexually transmitted diseases because three-quarters of them reported inconsistent or no condom use. In addition, most failed to disclose to their partners that they had had multiple partners or that they had tested positive for the HIV virus or other sexually transmitted diseases.

There is some good news. A recent survey from the University of California at Los Angeles reported that just over 42 percent of college freshmen endorse casual sex, down from 50 percent in 1975.[10] In surveying 348,465 freshmen throughout the country in their first week of classes, the researchers also reported that the "guzzling of beer" dropped to a record low, with less than 53 percent of the freshmen saying they drank beer occasionally or frequently.

The research is encouraging but does not reflect the anecdotal comments I heard from seniors who were resident assistants (RAs) in their college dormitories. One typical RA described the freshmen women as having "no clue in life. I see most of my students go out every night and they come back from bars, and I think to myself, Your parents are spending thousands of dollars for you to come here and drink and party and then do school-work. They party every night, not just Friday and Saturday."

Perhaps the UCLA research reflects the optimism of incoming students—they were interviewed during their first week—that they can handle the college social scene. Or perhaps students' attitudes are changing. Almost 30 percent of the freshmen surveyed in the UCLA study identified themselves as born-again Christians.

The RAs at another college told me they were concerned about the high incidence of eating disorders among the young women on their campus. Not only did they relate stories of "nobody eating" at the dining hall, one of them could name six residents in her section of thirty-four women (almost 20 percent) who had eating disorders. Another said, "I have forty-four girls in my section, and I know three [have eating disorders] for sure. Then there are the thin ones, and I'm sure some of them have an eating disorder." RAs generally do not know how to approach a student whom they suspect of having an eating disorder. The subject is not emphasized in their training sessions, as it should be. Early attention, both medical and psychological, to an eating disorder can avert a lifelong problem.

Colleges are not blind to their students' problems, and coun-seling facilities are expanding. A young woman who is addicted to alcohol or drugs or who has an eating disorder can find coun-seling and help on her campus if she reaches out for it. This is where a mother can help—by finding out all the resources avail-able in a school and encouraging, even escorting her daughter to the medical center.

New Role Models

During her college days, a daughter who is exposed to chal-lenging ideas, women professors, and feminist classmates may conclude that her mother is not her role model. "I would have been a different person if I didn't go to college," a woman in her midtwenties recalled. "I believed in women's rights, but I didn't have any sort of female model of independence until I went to college." A dedication to a cause, research project, or unusual person may take a daughter beyond her family's expectations for her. A daughter often senses that her mother worries about her exposure to different ideas. And, sometimes, a mother doesn't hesitate to state her opinion. One mother told a young woman that she didn't want her taking international courses because "she may go to that country and get a dread disease." All a young woman can do is reassure her mother that she will safeguard against the pitfalls that accompany any new adventure.

"Madly in Love with Shakespeare"

A great teacher, even just a good teacher, can inspire a young woman. When Jennifer registered for summer school as an exchange student on another campus, her mother warned her that she could not party all summer (as she liked to do), that she had to take a worthwhile course. At first Jennifer resented her mother's suggestion but realized that she had not been applying herself in class. Therefore, she carefully studied the courses available that summer, asked about the quality of the professors, and chose wisely. She fell "madly in love" with Shakespeare that summer and actually wrote a thank-you note to her mother for her advice, in spite of her complaint that she had to "work day and night" to survive in the class.

"You feel as though you've learned so much when you come out of here that you're just armed and ready to go," a senior said as she was discussing her progression from a "naïve" freshman to a seasoned senior. Her professors had stretched her mind and she applauded their efforts, although she admitted that she often protested the hard work and resisted their influence.

The College Network

The close college network of friends sustains women during the dark days of cramming for exams, writing all night, breaking up with boyfriends, or failing to get desired grades in important courses. With deaths of grandparents or parents, the breakup of parents' marriages, and the trauma of friends' crises, college friends form deep ties. They know each other well, have often lived with each other, and their friendships are formed with men as well as women.

According to research from Emory University, college women who are able to sustain a close network of friends and work in a college environment that provides equal opportunity to both men and women are less vulnerable to depression than high-school girls or adult women.[11] In many ways, a college campus offers the ideal setting for young women to develop their full potential in the company of, and on equal basis with, good male friends.

During the seventies and eighties, most all-male colleges opened their doors to women, so this generation of women, unlike their older sisters, did not have to integrate their schools. By the time they arrived in college, sororities and women's organizations were a vital part of the campus life. Lesbian women often could find organizations that welcomed them. Medical schools, law schools, and business schools were equally accessible to women and men. Women entered college with assurances that they would be treated equally.

This perception of equality is confirmed in a study conducted at the University of Texas that appraised students' attitude about gender-role equality, comparing the results of a seventies survey with the same survey conducted in the nineties.[12] College students in the nineties increasingly expected women and men to be treated equally in the workplace, home, and social settings (including either men or women proposing marriage)—a positive trend.

Not all women, however, experience equality in the classroom. But today they can do something about it. If a young
woman feels she is not recognized or that her accomplishments
are not acknowledged because she is a woman, she can bring her
grievance to the attention of a counselor, a school official, or a
friend. Merry, age 29, spoke about her experience in film school.
"I don't run into sexism now in the type of job I have, but I did
in college." Her professor was really "anti-women," and she was
one of the two remaining women in the class. She majored in
animation and in the final project teamed up with a male friend.
"The professor loved the cartoon we created and kept telling the
guy how great it was. My guy friend kept telling him it was my
idea and my work. At last my friend wrote to the professor,
making it clear that it was my project." That is a good friend.

I frequently heard from graduates that what they miss most
about college is the proximity of friends, both male and female.
"I don't have friends drop by like I did in college," a recent
graduate in California said. "My favorite thing about college was
people would just drop in [and] say, 'Hey what's going on?' or
'Let's hang out for a while.' Now we call and say, 'Come on
over and watch a movie.' You lose that wonderful easiness."

Computers also link students. Information about what's happening on campus, where friends will meet for a party, and what
class assignments are due connects students from across the
campus. Professors correspond with students, friends catch up
with friends, and students meet for the first time through E-mail.
Not only can parents reach their daughters directly through
E-mail, friends can stack up the messages, knowing that eventually they will read them.

Work Instead of College

College offers a slow transition to full-fledged adulthood, but it
certainly is not the only path. My older daughter spent only three

semesters at a performing arts college before pursuing a career in dance. Her transition from family and home to career and apartment was short. Many women move into careers directly after high school or technical school. When I interviewed a group of young hairdressers, I was impressed with how satisfied they seemed with their lives. They had met at a technical high school at age 15 and remained good friends.

When I asked them if they thought they differed from other young twenty-somethings who had been to college, one of them replied: "We don't expect things the way some 20-year-olds do. They expect someone to do everything for them, while we're more used to doing it ourselves. They expect the world to be handed to them on a platter because they grew up with parents who wanted to make sure they got the best of everything. If you keep giving and giving and giving to your kids, they're just going to keep wanting and wanting and wanting." She did not resent her peers who were still dependent on their parents' income, but she thought they were immature.

Women who enter the workforce immediately after or shortly after high school learn how to budget their money and their time. Retail stores provide abundant jobs (at low pay) for high-school graduates, and some store clerks told me they were in serious retail careers, hoping to manage a store in the future. They didn't think their lack of a college degree hindered their ability to sell or to manage. And they knew that if they were serious about a career, they would be rewarded.

When I asked Lisa, a 20-year-old, if she wanted to be boss, she immediately said yes and was very confident that she would become a manager soon. After working at a store for three months, she had been promoted to manager-in-training and then shortly after that to assistant manger. Lisa plans on managing a store with heavy customer traffic because her salary will depend on the volume produced at the store and her goal is to make money. She does not envy those who have gone to college. She quit college after one semester. "I was so sick of the college scene," she said, "where you drink yourself into oblivion and someone has to babysit you, and that would always end up being me 'cause I don't drink. So I was the one making sure they got to bed okay without puking all over themselves or going off with some random guy. I got sick of that really fast."

A friend who worked in retail with Lisa commented in a similar vein. "I got tired of the college scene too, and I'm one of those people who likes to party, but I have a little more self-control than most people. I saw myself without a reason to be there and [saw college as] a waste of everyone's money and I said, 'Forget it' and came home."

Other working women mentioned various reasons for not attending college or not staying in college. Some, like my older daughter, were eager to get on with their careers. My daughter recognized that a career in modern dance required early commitment. At age 18, after three semesters at a performing arts college and many auditions, she received an offer to dance with a modern dance company. I'll never forget her excitement when she greeted us with the news. She was going to dance with a company that even paid for rehearsal time—a major accomplishment for an 18-year-old.

Others leave school because they miss their families or boyfriends. Leigh recalled: "I remember my parents' reaction when I went to college. It wasn't a happy one. I was the only one of the family who left to go to college, and they had a tough time dealing with it. I remember a couple of times I walked in and my parents were crying, and I tried to ignore it, but I'd walk away and go to my room and cry. My school was only forty-five minutes away, but I didn't live at home. I came home every weekend because my boyfriend was here and I missed my mother's cooking so much." She left college after one semester.

A young hairdresser also reported that missing her boyfriend brought her back home. She attended college for two years. "It really was difficult partly because of my boyfriend," she said. "My heart wasn't in school. I worked as a hairdresser before I left and I was used to having money, and I was broke in school and didn't really have an interest. I was doing it because my parents wanted me to, but I really didn't have a purpose to continue."

Whether the motivation to work is a passion for the arts or the desire to make money or dissatisfaction with college, young women who work full-time after high school have many options. Some may return to school at a later time to pursue another career, as my daughter did. Many of these young women, at least during their decade of the twenties, have an advantage over college women—they know where they want to go.

"I Appreciate Her So Much More": The Relationship Changes

The misunderstandings and turmoil of the adolescent daughter-mother relationship seem to evaporate during a daughter's years at college, especially if she is living away from home. Researchers from the University of Michigan found that living away was associated with greater independence, support, and mutual respect between the college student and her parents.[13] College students who lived at home and commuted to class were more likely to continue viewing the relationship negatively, probably because they felt constraints similar to those of their high-school days.

When I asked a group of seniors in a residential college if their attitudes toward their mothers had changed during their four years in school, they all admitted feeling very different now than they had felt in freshman year. Joyce, for example, used to have a lot of resentment toward her mom. "I can't say I blamed her for my parents' divorce, but I definitely saw my dad's side," she said. "My mom's a very spiritual person and my dad wasn't, and I resented her for focusing so much on that and not on family life." Joyce used to say that she was never going to be like her mother, but now she is very conscious of the ways they are similar. Even her career goals are now very much in line with those of her mother (who is a doctor). "I don't know if I'm turning into my mother," Joyce said. "But I've come to appreciate her so much more and understand her as a whole person so much more. I think it has a lot to do with distance, and I think it has a lot to do with my developmental stage."

All in the room agreed with Joyce that their new stage contributed to a better understanding of their mothers and therefore a better relationship.

Fran commented: "Our relationship has changed because I've matured. My mother used to call me all the time. We still talk, not as much, but I've gotten closer to her. When I go home, we talk about things that matter in my life and in her life." Fran feels, however, that there's a limit to their conversation. Her mother is not interested in the world events and issues that concern Fran. She lovingly calls her mother a "gossiper," and they talk about friends and family only.

Although Fran's mother did not attend college and is not particularly interested in her class work, Fran has achieved a "transition to equality" with her mother and is able to view the world through her mother's eyes. They do not have the same intellectual interests (Fran wants to be a lawyer), but they have found companionship and love in gossiping about and concern for family.

Anne smiled as she described her change in attitude: "At 13 we were far apart. She was the same but I was into the 'me' stage, but now we're like best friends. I can call up my mom and tell her just about anything. When you're young, you think friends are the most important thing. You realize as you go through life that you lose friends and get others, but your family is always there. They don't leave. They're constantly there for you."

Moving On

When September of senior year rolls around, most women are restless and ready to move on. Their excitement is boundless. As one senior explained to me in October: "I think this summer I got on a power trip. I don't know if it's a power trip really, but I just decided that I want to get out and make my own money for a while. My job this summer was going out on sales calls with these businessmen, and I like the idea of doing that. I think we're ready to graduate and move on to a job or grad school."

But by the time May arrives, they are less eager. They realize that the close-knit family of friends will be departing for all corners of the country and, sometimes, the globe. The same feeling of anxiety that they felt as they departed for college returns. Uncertainty prevails on the college campus. Job rejection slips ("ding" letters) are posted on the bulletin boards. Suddenly graduate schools and volunteer organizations look appealing. Some seniors make plans to travel, to take time off before looking for a "real" job, while others seek temp or waitressing jobs until they figure out what they really want to do. And many will respond, "I don't know" when they are asked what they are going to do when they graduate.

I discovered the worst question one could ask a senior was, "What are you going to do after graduation?" The seniors who had received a job offer or acceptance to graduate school or admission to the peace corps would talk about their future without being asked. The others volunteered information when they felt comfortable enough to vocalize their lack of plans.

Seniors share a sense of sorrow that they are leaving the security of a campus that has nurtured them during important formative years and a sense of grief that they no longer will experience the closeness of their friends. They have lived by an academic calendar since kindergarten, and their activities have been structured within an academic environment. Now they will be responsible for themselves—and mothers can't help.

"I felt a slight distancing from my mother at this stage," a 26-year-old said as she looked back on her senior year. "She was married before she finished school. I felt she couldn't relate to my experiences: the stress of interviewing and entering the fast-paced business world. I felt she had no advice to offer me. I felt very alone, graduating with no job and no one to counsel me."

A mother may not have undergone the same transition to adulthood as her daughter and not fully understand her daughter's dilemma. But she can acknowledge that her daughter's next years will be very different than her own decade of the twenties and support her daughter fully. The daughter's next few years will not be easy as she must choose among seemingly unlimited choices, a difficult task any time but particularly daunting in new settings without the old network of friends. And because, unlike her mother, the daughter does not expect to get married quickly, her career takes on added significance as she contemplates supporting herself for the next years. She will turn to her mother for advice, but what she wants is a quiet supporter.

By the end of college, whether a daughter's job is settled or remains uncertain, whether a mother and daughter truly understand each other or not, both must move on and adjust to their first years of living independently of each other.

2

The First Years Out

Daughters

Mothers

Reality

A daughter's empty bedroom constantly reminds a mother that her daughter now is an adult and she must refocus her parenting energies. And a daughter, when she leaves her familiar home and enters the working world, knows she also must refocus: find a job, an apartment, and roommates.

The uncertainty about what lies ahead is heard in the voices of both mothers and daughters. "What will I do?" they lament. Of course, a daughter's search is different from her mother's. She is willing to try many careers, live in new cities, and travel to far-off countries. That is unlikely to be her mother's quest. A daughter has a lifetime to form and fulfill her dreams. Her mother has a shorter time line and family or work obligations she cannot abandon.

Daughters

Many daughters are not finding what they expected in their immediate postcollege years. Joanie and a group of her friends in their early twenties gathered one Saturday morning in her sunny living room, a small space that captured the only natural light available on her city block. Across the street, workers could be heard erecting a new building that soon would block Joanie's ray of sunlight. As she and her friends talked about their frustrations and joys, I was conscious of how much her apartment differed from a college dorm. The careful arrangement created a motif of comfort and coziness, yet the sparsely furnished apartment reflected its occupant's new status as a working woman. Joanie earns enough money to live alone, and for that she is unique among her friends. But as they exchanged stories about their first years out of school, Joanie and her friends' experiences echoed each other.

"When we graduated," Joanie commented woefully, "we weren't prepared." Her friends nodded in agreement. They felt "lost," as one women described her mood when she embarked on what many people had told her would be some of the best years of her life. They imagined fabulous jobs, new exciting friends, and an active social life. To outsiders, they might look successful. They have jobs, roommates, apartments, and friends.

Yet these young women are not finding the satisfaction or the fun they had been told to expect. They often contrast their single working life to college. One, two, even three years out of school, they admit that they were ready to graduate, yet they miss everything about college life. College had provided a well-defined structure, a schedule to follow, and academic goals to accomplish. They had shared rooms with good friends who understood them. They could go to a social event any night of the week and always were confident of meeting potential boyfriends. "Oh my God, I miss it so much," remarked one recent graduate. "I don't miss being a student, but the lifestyle is so nice."

Just as most mothers miss the excitement of children, their daughters miss the tumultuous life of college. Now on their own, often with roommates they have met through remote contacts, the early-twenties women despair over the gap between their dreams of an incredible first job and great apartment, and the reality of their boring jobs and cramped apartments. At first I thought that Joanie's friends were having trouble adjusting to their new low-budget living conditions and missed the relative luxury of their family homes. But as I interviewed young graduates, I realized that many of the women feel a pall over their lives. Lots of well-employed, underemployed, and not-yet-employed women are experiencing a discontent, a restlessness that indicates this is not what they bargained for. As one woman said: "I had this cushion under me for four years. Then I was shoved to go figure out what to do. I can't depend on anyone. This is something you have to do on your own. It's scary."

The word *scary* appeared again and again in our conversations. The first years out of college are tough as young women adjust to life, often without the intimacy of family or old friends. For many, looking for grown-up, real-life employment is terrifying. In their senior year, they put all their energy into finishing college and enjoying the remaining time with close friends; the question of "what next" wasn't a priority. It didn't help matters that they had no clear idea of what they wanted to do. Now, as graduates, they want the "right" job in the "right" location, but "what and where" must still be determined.

"What Am I Going to Do?"

The question "What am I going to do?" disrupts a young woman's view of herself. Throughout her adolescent and college years, she explored the question "Who am I?" and believed that as long as she fulfilled her role as daughter, friend, girlfriend, student, she was on the right path. Even as her mother told her, "You can do anything you want," she knew that a primary "thing" she wanted was to love and be loved. She yearned to keep connected to family and friends. When a young woman enters the world of work, she realizes it offers opportunities for money, security, or status, but not necessarily for friendship. Work does not reward her for maintaining relationships and sometimes does just the opposite: Work moves her far away from friends. "Doing" had been incidental to her concept of herself; now what she does is primary. "We all talk about what we do, but it has nothing to do with me and where I'm going with my life," complained one 24-year-old.

Back in the apartment, Anne, one of Joanie's closest friends, described how she has worked in a couple of different career-type jobs but hasn't found one she likes. As she talked about her frustrations, she enumerated her wishes. "The thing I wish I had done earlier was talk to more people who had professional careers because I don't have a strong female role model. I wish I had a better understanding about a career. I wish I had known what questions to ask. I wish someone had told me what I needed to know. I wish I had a better understanding that the choices I was making at 21 or 22 are not necessarily permanent."

Anne's mother, who does not work outside the home, does not offer a career role model for her. Many mothers of young graduates stayed at home to take care of children, and if they worked outside the home, they worked part-time. Only 32.7 percent of all women between the ages of 25 and 54 work full-time, and only 4.2 percent of women over the age of 55 work full-time.[1] Young women told me they are finding new role models, women in their thirties and forties, in the offices and agencies where they work.

The first year out of college is the hardest for those who did not find employment before they graduated and who consequently moved back with their parents. Joanie's friend Margaret typifies the unemployed scenario of the postcollege blues. She is tired of hearing people, especially her parents, tell her how lucky she is to have so many options. She doesn't think she is lucky, only stressed. "It's a huge time of decision making," she said, "and nobody acknowledges that. I was intimidated by any decision I had to face." Confronted with too many decisions, she withdrew from making any that would dramatically change her life. She moved back with her parents.

Because her parents had not gone to college, they didn't think they had any "connections" and felt inadequate to advise her about the job application process. Their bewilderment and frustration made Margaret feel worse. Her parents had sacrificed to send her to school, and now she was not producing. The longer she stayed with her parents, the more paralyzed she became. Not until a friend called and asked her to help with a project did she gain the courage to apply for a part-time job in an art supply shop nine months after graduation.

Imagine the distress that Margaret's mother felt as she watched her educated daughter withdraw from friends who were working and on their own. She feared she had passed on her own feelings of inadequacy to Margaret and was relieved when her daughter at last found a job that would get her out of the house and mingling with others. Margaret is approaching 24 and continues to hold a part-time job. It is time for her to start supporting herself, even if it is part-time and not one that lives up to Margaret's or her own expectations.

At some point a young unemployed or underemployed woman must be forced to overcome her inertia and take a job, any job, to stimulate her energy and focus her goals. Having a job helps her clarify what she does or does not like in her work. By supporting her without expecting anything in return, her parents are sapping her strength. An unemployed daughter living at home feels natural and is often fun for parents, but she should contribute to her upkeep and keep searching for a job—daily.

Margaret's dilemma is by no means unique. According to a recent report, the number of 20- to 24-year-old women in the labor force is declining.[2] Economists offer various reasons for the decline, including women remaining in school or returning to school, but from my discussions with young women, I found that some women are delaying their entrance into the world of work because they cannot choose a field or they fear being rejected so they find some excuse not to apply. Others are unable to picture themselves working a nine-to-five office job, so they search for some other type of work. Still others accept volunteer or apprentice positions to experience various professions.

"I got over the feeling of being lost," said Laura, age 23, who had emerged from her first-year blues, "because my friends and I were all saying the same thing. We didn't know where we were going with our careers. We didn't know what we were doing with our lives. We didn't know what we were doing with our boyfriends. I said, 'Thank God there are 13 of us in this world who feel the same way because misery loves company.' For me it was an unbelievable experience. I hated the transition, but you've got to take control of your life."

Taking control of life means taking risks. Joanie's friends who are paralyzed must be willing to change jobs, reach for higher levels, or move to different cities. I don't think they will be in charge of their lives unless they explore different types of careers, and they can't do that by sitting on a couch. Friends and family may help a young woman in her search, but only she can take charge of her life.

Taking Control

In contrast to women like Margaret who linger at the threshold of commitment to work, others take control and pursue employment opportunities near home or far away. Taking control presents a challenge, particularly when a woman is fresh from the security of school and "dropped at the doorstep to the rest of my life," as one woman described her dilemma. Each recent graduate with whom I spoke managed to find her own way to bring some order to her life. While every story is unique, six women typify the many ways young women approach the world of work.

Alyson recalls that she took her first job quickly because she needed the income and hated interviewing. At first she was thrilled when she was hired by an ad agency to sell space, but she quickly realized that the salary would not pay for an apartment in Los Angeles. She would have to commute from her parents' home. She called her four-hour round-trip commute her "second job." After a year of selling ads, she had accumulated enough money to move into a minuscule apartment with two roommates. Her success as a sales rep gave her the courage to seek another position which promised more money, but her choice turned out to be disastrous; the company was run by "creeps." Again, she felt she had options and through an employment agency obtained a job that she is now turning into a career path. Her entry-level pay scale prompted her to look around the company for a better-paying job. When she saw a vacancy in an area she liked, she applied for the opening. Although the job was posted for a person with a more technical background, Alyson convinced her superiors to give her a chance.

"I was stuck faxing and copying," she said. "I didn't want to tell the management that wasn't what I came to do. I pretty much saw another job and went for it. Rather than lashing out, saying, 'Look, I didn't come here to do copying,' I did it in a more positive way. I said I'd take it on." After receiving the promotion, she returned the next day to negotiate for a higher salary, which she received.

How did Alyson, who initially was as confused about a career as any graduate, decide to take control and try to advance in the business world?

Alyson is motivated partly by her parents' pride in her and partly by her financial needs. Alyson and her mother are very close and speak on the phone daily. Both her parents, she says, really admire her. They each have routine jobs; her mother "hates her job" and works only because she needs the income. Her mother is impressed that Alyson speaks up to supervisors, works late hours, and is committed to a good career. Alyson herself sometimes wonders if she has reached too far. Will she succeed in her new position? Her network of family and friends is recognizing her ambition and providing further motivation to succeed.

Because Alyson had borrowed money to pay for college, she could not postpone her job search after graduation. Today, many students are dependent on financial aid, part-time employment, and/or loans to pay their college expenses. In the fall of 1996, 33 percent of students entering college chose the college because of the financial aid package, and 41 percent of freshmen held part-time jobs to help them pay for tuition.[3] A Midwestern college reported that nearly half of its students borrow as much as $5,150 each year.[4] In Alyson's case, she had obtained a small loan to cover the expenses not paid by financial aid or her parents. These loans, repaid monthly, are obligations like rent or credit cards. Alyson's determination to negotiate for a higher salary was motivated by her need for money to pay off her loans.

Other women are propelled by emotional rather than financial needs to seek better employment. Pam, a flight attendant, squeezed in next to me on a crowded two-hour flight from Chicago. Caught in the bad weather, she was rushing to catch her next assignment on a flight out of New York. Pam had worked as a dental assistant in a suburban office her first year out of college and lived with her divorced mother. One weekend she flew to Atlanta to visit college friends, and the trip redirected her life. At the end of a great weekend when her friends urged her to move and join them in Atlanta, she burst into tears. The weekend had pierced her routine. She contrasted her dull existence of living with her mother and working in a children's dentist's office with her friends' exciting life in a major city. When her mother met Pam at the plane, she began crying again. Distressed by her daughter's tears, Pam's mother asked her what she really would like to do. At first she wailed, "I don't know," but then she thought how much she enjoyed traveling and told her mother she wanted to be a flight attendant. Within two weeks, with her mother's encouragement, she filled out an application and was hired. She loves her job and has never looked back. Her mother did not hesitate to support her even though she knew that they would not see each other as much. She put her daughter's interests above her own.

Andie took control of her life in another way. Because she had volunteered at a children's agency during college, she knew she liked working with children, but in what capacity? She joined a volunteer corp that supplied assistants to understaffed social agencies throughout the country. Andie lived with other volunteers in Seattle and received a small stipend. Working with disturbed adolescents and living with three women she didn't know was not easy at first. "I cried the whole way to Seattle," she said. "I thought, Why am I leaving friends? Why am I going to Seattle where I don't know anyone? It was the first time I had gone anywhere without knowing a soul."

When her year's commitment was over, Andie reflected back on the benefits. "The women I lived with were different than my other friends, and they forced me to think about life in a different way, live in a different way, think and feel in a different way. It was one of the best years of my life." She decided to continue working with adolescents and plans to return to graduate school for a master's in social work. Because of her devotion to her family, Andie found that living on her own, away from her family, taught her a lot about independence. But she does not want to always live far away from her family and eventually will practice in a nearby city.

Many young women search for internships in order to experience possible careers. Our younger daughter had studied Latin

America and human rights in college and wanted to become familiar with the many organizations involved in that area. She took an internship at the Carter Center in Atlanta, where she had the opportunity to work with dedicated professionals while waitressing at night and on weekends to pay her expenses. Her internship in the department that monitored elections throughout the world exposed her to the complexities of international politics. Then she interned at Amnesty International, organizing volunteers and special projects until she obtained a full-time position with a human rights agency in Guatemala. Six months of internships solidified her determination to work with oppressed people and enabled her to make an informed decision about a career.

An internship with the Democratic party paid off for Alexandra. "The first year out of college was not my worst year because I got into what I wanted to do, and now I feel like I'm on the right track," she said. "I waitressed while I was interning, and that scared me. I had nightmares about being a waitress for the next 20 years." But her volunteering during a state representative's campaign led to a job in his office when he won the election. Now she has "a job, an income, and feels independent." And soon she hopes to have an apartment of her own because she claims her mother has forgotten that she is 23 and treats her like a high-school girl. "I have regulations and have to share the car," she said with disbelief.

Toni took a different tack. When she told her mother that she wanted to take a year off after college to figure out what she wanted to do, her mother readily agreed, with one condition. She had to pay her own way. Her year of "reflection" took place in Jackson, Wyoming, where she taught ski classes to young children, waitressed at two restaurants, and sold ads for the local newspaper. By the end of the ski season, she knew that she did not want to live forever in a resort area but definitely liked working in journalism. She moved to San Francisco, where she writes for a magazine and now thinks she will remain there. Her mother, who lives alone, wonders if she should have encouraged Toni's first venture away from home. Although they talk often on the phone, she misses her frequent visits.

These six women took control of their lives by taking chances, each in her own way. They were scared. They cried. But they risked change. Alyson risked changing jobs and spoke up when she spotted an opening. Pam risked change and stepped completely away from her secure job as a dental assistant to fly, trading irregular schedules and nights away from home for great travel opportunities. Andie risked leaving a comfortable and known location and friends and took a year to test a career possibility that led to a solid career path. Our daughter's six months as an intern was the catalyst for her decision to work for the indigenous people's rights in Guatemala where she knew no one. Alexandra found her passion in politics but had to spend seven months volunteering and waitressing before she realized her dream of a political job. And Toni, during her year off, discovered her interest in journalism and moved to a city that would offer job opportunities in the field.

Speaking Out

Even graduates whose talents and interests are a match with the job market also must find the right company, the right atmosphere. Many women in their early twenties are not willing to endure a harsh, competitive environment. They dream of working in a company that respects their ideas. Marta, who comes from a first-generation American family and still speaks Italian with her mother, attracted many employers because of her math skills. However, she hated the way she was treated in her first "real" job with a large financial firm. Her fourteen- to fifteen-hour workday was monitored closely by an unpleasant supervisor. She was not allowed to leave her desk, even for a cup of coffee, or take a walk during lunch break. She was the only female trainee in the office. Her supervisor was pleased because she made good phone contacts and was bringing in more business. However, her ability brought her more attention and more monitoring of her time.

Marta endured as long as she could because she was well paid, needed the money, and her family was proud of her. But her patience ended when she was invited to the company Christmas party but was asked to wear a red jacket and be in charge of parking cars. She confronted her employers and left. Although she worked for the firm only four months, she learned what she did not like and the limits of her tolerance. She was hired by another brokerage house closer to where she lived. The atmosphere is entirely different in this office. The employees work together to solve problems and help each other whenever they can.

Marta struck me as a very strong young woman who will advance rapidly in her company. Although she has been out of school less than a year (and lives with her closely knit family), she knows the type of company she wants. She has prepared for this job since her childhood when she took over her family's finances during her father's illness. She is determined to succeed, but because she works in a male-dominated business, she also is realistic. She realizes that few women attain partnerships in their firms, so she wonders about her future.

Many young women think that once they secure that first job, they will be set. Marta certainly did. But as she discovered, the first job may not be the right one; indeed, chances are it won't be. Choosing the correct career is important, but finding the right company or organization within that business will take time.

Young women allow themselves more flexibility in adjusting to work life than do young men, who often are expected to settle in and advance sooner than their female cohorts. Perhaps mothers and fathers of daughters are more tolerant of "time out" than parents of sons. Or perhaps daughters show their disappointment and discouragement about a job more openly than sons, so parents are more sympathetic with their daughters and encourage them to keep searching for a job they like.

"I Love My Job"

Not all young women are unhappy with their first jobs. The exceptions include three young women who met while working on a high-tech magazine on the West Coast. When they talk about their jobs, they use the word *love* and *our*, an unusual combination to describe employment. "I love our company," said one. "I'm so glad I'm working there. It's an amazing experience. I don't know if I want to do it for ten years, but it's a fun job. You can work out during lunch for an hour and a half and come back, and no one will check a watch. You're friends with the other people." She had worked for a temp agency that sent her to the same job everyday for five months. She complained that there was "no energy" in that office. "The people were old and miserable and unhappy," she recalled. "It was awful. I dreaded going there. I don't dread going to work now at all."

Each one of these recent graduates realizes how lucky she is to work in a young, fun environment. Two of them had moved away from their families on the opposite coast to experience living on their own. They talk lovingly of their families and how much their mothers miss them. They don't plan on spending their lives away from their families, but for now, they are willing to see their families a couple of times a year.

These young women work hard and willingly because they like the people in the office. "It's a robotic job," said one enthusiastically. "It takes a lot of energy." They also appreciate the respect that is shown to all employees, and they especially like meeting the other young members of the staff.

Another woman has worked in an insurance company since her graduation and also thinks her company is "terrific": "I love it. They are rewarding me, and it feels like family. It sounds corny, but the company attracts a terrific type of person." Because this young woman is alienated from her family and at the moment finds her mother unapproachable, her job is replacing her family.

From my interviews with young women, I concluded that if a company rewards their hard work, they will produce and become valued employees. But if they don't feel respected or their talents are not appreciated, they will leave. I sensed that they would not hesitate to quit an unsatisfactory job— although the prospect of interviewing for another job tempers their decisions.

This generation of women was brought up believing they could do everything. They want the chance to prove it, and they have the full backing of their mothers, who speak proudly of their accomplishments. One of the rewards these young women expect is a salary large enough to live a comfortable life in a good apartment. Because of the paucity of good-paying entry-level jobs, they may have to wait awhile for that reward. But they are impatient and restless.

Adjusting to a New City

"Why did you choose to live here?" I asked young women who had moved from one part of the country to another. Large cities such as Boston, New York, Chicago, Atlanta, Dallas, San Francisco, Los Angeles, Seattle act like magnets attracting recent graduates.

Unlike their mothers, who may not have left their parents' home until marriage or moved to an apartment in the same town or a nearby city, many of these young women are willing to move anywhere. Not all of them think they will live in their new city forever. Many told me they eventually will move back to be near their families. But for the first few years of work, they feel free to move from one end of the country to another. One expressed the feelings of many when she said, "I don't want to have to think I have to keep living here [her hometown]. I don't want to be tied down."

When I interviewed women on the West Coast, the exodus seemed to lean from east to west. The West promised a less formal atmosphere at work, opportunities to meet new people, and proximity to great recreational areas. Then when I interviewed women on the East Coast, I saw the reverse trend. "Almost all of my friends on the West Coast have moved east," I was told by a graduate student.

Laurie used her first tax refund to pay for a vacation in Chicago. Within a week she had decided to move to that city, even though the only people she knew there were her aunt and uncle. She liked the atmosphere and was bored with her job in the East. Within a month and a half she "was in a normal living situation in a new city." She immediately joined a gym and worked two jobs so she could meet people. She said her dad was "sad" and her mother "dismayed," but they talk on the phone almost every day. Their long conversations have eased the transition.

As I talked with these women who move around the country—and the world—I thought about their mothers, who may see their daughters only a few times a year and miss them deeply (as I did). Whether a daughter is living in a nearby large city or in a faraway land, the fear for her security is the same. One mother told me her daughter was living in a very "bad" neighborhood but would not move because "she is saving the world block by block."

A Place to Live

Finding a job goes hand in hand with searching for a place to live. Although some young women return to their parents' home after graduation, their stay usually is short because they want to be with their own age group, sharing an apartment, however small, and pooling resources.

Mothers can rightfully be concerned about their daughters' choice of dwelling, and I empathize with them. When our older daughter pursued her dance career, she lived in an old building surrounded by burned-out buildings and next to a small park known for its homeless people and drug dealers. I admired her determination to live on her income, yet I cringed as we dropped her off at her apartment. Her safety concerned us, but her ambition inspired us. Our other daughter lived in Guatemala for three years amid a background of poverty, roadblocks, and military skirmishes. We were proud of her work with human rights but prayed for her safety.

Because parents are so concerned about security, many will subsidize their daughters' rent during their first years out of college so they can live in safe neighborhoods. Usually the rents in the major cities that attract a young population are too high to be covered by a single woman, so she must have roommates. One young woman slept on a couch for a year before she could find an apartment with a vacant bedroom. While the women search for apartments in which each may have her own bedroom, compromises often have to be made.

Because women in their early twenties usually don't live in their dream apartments, attitudes about their living quarters range from despair to acceptance. One woman who moved into the city to be independent and reduce her commuting time initially told me she hated her apartment. But when she said she lived only three blocks from the subway and loved her roommate, she began to extol its merits. Her main complaint was its size, "a tiny box, and I'm going nuts with [the lack of] storage space." Many thought that when they left the cramped college dormitory rooms, they would find space for clothes, books, and makeup. However, they share tiny apartments with one, two, or three other women, and sometimes men. No one has enough space.

Women who are willing to live on the fringes of a city have more options. I interviewed a group of women who live in a large home in the hills surrounding Los Angeles. Five people, a combination of men and women, share the spacious house, and each has put her or his own touch to the house. They help one another find jobs (they all are in the film industry), meet friends, and organize housework. I was impressed with their generosity toward each other and their guests.

Some mothers can't wait to decorate their daughters' apartments and often redo furniture that may have otherwise been discarded. When daughters are willing, mothers with a decorative eye enjoy shopping with them to make small apartments more livable. Those lucky mothers spoke of the fun they had helping their daughters move into apartments.

But many young women want to create their own style. Although they appreciate their mothers' offers, they and their roommates want to find and decorate apartments themselves. They are striking out on their own, away from their mothers' daily influence—and decorating ideas.

Do Mothers Understand?

No matter which city or country a daughter has chosen as the site of her first "real" job, she and her friends share an outlook that sounds familiar. "If I can make it here, I can make it any-where," claimed one recent graduate as her friends nodded their heads in agreement. The challenges of the early twenties: a first job, a first apartment, and a new city—will they "make it?"

These young women are testing themselves, and the testing

includes adjusting to a city and a lifestyle that is not and probably never was their mothers' lifestyle. Can their mothers understand? Some daughters assume their mothers sympathize with the frustrations of the first years out of school, but others wonder if their mothers, coming from different experiences, could possibly understand.

"I had disdain for my mother when I was first out of school," a young woman (who is very fond of her mother) told me. "She never had to search for a job, earn her own living, anguish over what she was going to do, or cope with meeting different types of people. She couldn't understand."

Her mother, she said, wanted to understand but could not grasp the complexities of her daughter's life. But at last her mother learned to listen and not continually offer advice, a major step that led to their good adult relationship.

Mothers

The search that a woman undertakes when her last child leaves home is not unlike her daughter's. A mother also is entering a new stage, midlife, which makes her question her normal routine and reevaluate her life and her relationships. Her daughter's absence sparks thoughts about the future.

"When my daughter left, I spent most of the spring mourning, and it's still very fresh," Martha, age 49, said. "It's not that I threaded my life completely around her because I worked all the time, but it really hit between the eyes—boom. My mother says, 'You loved them with open hands. It's time to let them go and soar.' All those platitudes, but I think to myself— that bedroom is so empty."

Daughters would agree with their grandmothers, "It's time to let them go." They want their mothers to acknowledge their departure and to move on to activities in their own lives. They don't want to worry about them. But daughters also want their mothers to stay interested in them, to keep in close contact, to be a support. Young women may still critique their mothers but now with more love and understanding than they had as adolescents.

Lucy, age 23, is living at home temporarily while looking for a good job. She can't believe that her mother keeps talking about her own need to be treated like an adult. "She's 53 and I'm 23, and I'm saying the same thing my mother is," Lucy said in desperation. "I think we're actually going through the same thing. I don't know if she's going through it because I'm around, or I'm going through it because she's around." Lucy has caught the full blast of her mother's restlessness as her mother faces midlife with a grown daughter back in the house.

Martha, with a part-time job and full-time husband, still receives "helpful" suggestions from her daughters. She recalled her daughters asking her, "What are you going to do?" Martha would reply, "What do you mean, 'What am I going to do?' I'm doing what I'm going to do." She thinks they want her to be "stimulated and stimulating—no pinning doilies on the couches."

"My daughters want to reinvent me," laughed another woman as she described her two executive-type daughters' wholehearted efforts to make her change her style of hair and dress, her place of work, and to take up cycling. Her daughters are paying attention to her, not ignoring her as they settle into apartments and form new circles of friends. They want their mother to be her own person, to rediscover herself now that they have left the house.

Most mothers want that for themselves. They look forward to the free time made available by departing children to develop other interests. They also look forward to expressing themselves openly without worrying about hurting anyone's feelings. "My mother's becoming so assertive, she's becoming a bitch," a young woman laughingly reported. "She's cussing all the time. I love it."

Finding Her Own Voice

When mothers finally realize that their daughters' apartments are their real homes, that their daughters are postponing marriage, and that grandchildren look more distant than ever, they begin to look to their own futures. Many fruitful years lie ahead (a possible thirty years or more), and they have plenty of time to fulfill their own dreams and plans. Some bury themselves in more work at the office. Many return to school. Others apprentice themselves to artists, find a mentor in a new job, make new friends, volunteer for causes they think worthwhile, or run for political office. Four of the local officials in my town are women who entered politics in midlife. These women are following their aspirations, finding their own voices, and looking beyond their daughters' empty rooms.

Women who have strived to be the ideal mother find relief in just being themselves. Cathy, a 52-year-old woman whose youngest daughter is in college, is exploring new interests, including spending some time studying Eastern spirituality. She explained how her studies were changing her life. "I used to pretend I was the same old me. It recently occurred to me, no, this is who I am. This is what I'm interested in. Whenever my husband would say, 'What happened to good old Cathy?' I would go back to my old self. But now I know this is who I am."

Noreen, in her midfifties, talks daily with her daughter in a distant city and feels a new freedom to say what she likes. "I feel like I'm on a total high," Noreen, an owner of a small business, exclaimed as we talked about daughters. "My daughter has moved to the coast, and I now have this incredible revisionist attitude that we were the total "Brady Bunch." It makes me feel good. I look at my career and look at what my goals are, and my goals are definitely to feel good. I'm trying to figure how to do that 'cause my schedule still keeps me running as fast as I can. I don't have to accomplish. I don't feel that right now. I do what I do, and I belong to what I belong to, and I give what I give."

Noreen's enthusiasm is catching, and everyone can imagine the advantage of reexamining the family through the rosy glasses of revisionist history. Rather than focusing on the difficult times of raising a daughter, Noreen chooses to put her own twist on the story. All their days were fun, and her children were angels. Maybe she is unrealistic, but Noreen's attitude propels her to happily plan her next stage. She may hand over some of the responsibilities of her business so she can pursue what makes her "feel good."

Many of her peers would agree that getting "old" gives a woman permission to be who she is. "I'm now comfortable at being an expert," said a psychologist who teaches and supervises young psychologists and also continues her successful practice. Although she still works four nights a week, she and her husband now take longer vacations and "see who they want to see"—a great advantage to the empty room. Midlife moms are coming into their own.

Becoming One's Self

Women's desire to "find" themselves after their daughters have gone on to their new lives expresses itself in diverse ways. Many women want to become more involved in their work (whether it is full-time, part-time, or volunteer). Some want to change jobs, find jobs, or quit working, now that college payments aren't due. Because of their experiences in work or community activities, mothers have an advantage over their daughters, who are searching at the same time to establish their sense of self.

Mothers have dabbled in many areas. Many women told me that they would just "love to do more of what I love to do." Some never had the time to explore their talents because family and work took priority. But when they look back on their lives, they often remember a hobby or interest they enjoyed in their youth. They determine to try that activity again.

"I like to write poetry," Marge, a 51-year-old executive said. "I had a poem published once, but I have had no time to spend on poetry in the last years. I would love to go back to school and take courses in exotic things. I love to read. I love to travel. I love to bird-watch. I say to myself, 'When am I going to do these things?' Maybe I'll stop working full-time." Cutting back in their work hours or finding part-time jobs presents an appealing option to many midlife mothers whose income is no longer needed for college tuition.

When I was interviewing a group of mothers in the Midwest, Denise, a dynamic yet calm-looking woman, told me how her present work with flexible hours has evolved from her paid and volunteer jobs during the past fifteen years.

"I've enjoyed every stage of life," Denise said. "What I think is open to women at this point is the opportunity to begin to explore other parts of ourselves." Denise was a teacher for a number of years. She loves to teach, and her interest in the environment led her to study Chinese herbal medicine; now she has a practice in this field and teaches workshops on both Chinese and Western herbs. "I've had a few careers and they all relate, but this is a different stage of my life and work and it's great."

Denise believes that her 26-year-old daughter considers her a role model. Her daughter is a social worker living in the South, and they talk frequently. Denise detects a sense of pride in her daughter's voice when she asks about her mother's practice.

Many women find themselves entering careers they had thought about years before. When I asked some mothers to tell me about their working lives when they were their daughters' ages, they were, at first, reluctant to dwell on their own lives and consistently undervalued what they had done. But as they talked about their present work, either paid or volunteer, I could see that the interests they pursued in their twenties were guiding their involvement in midlife.

When Jacqui told me about her early working career, I saw many parallels between her past career, her present-day work, and, interestingly, her daughter's profession. During college, she majored in political science, international affairs, and studied languages. Jacqui's first job was working in the press office of a political campaign, writing, contacting people, setting up speaking arrangements. Her career progressed in the direction she had planned when she moved over to a major daily newspaper and worked with the news bureau, occasionally covering the United Nations and writing feature articles with a byline. "I learned so much," she said, looking back. She stopped working outside the home when her children were born.

When I asked Jacqui to tell me what she is doing now that her daughters are grown, she told me that she is working with a refugee group, having organized a community and now a nationwide effort to help refugees. She writes a newsletter, articles, and press releases. "I realized I could write," Jacqui said, "and it is fun. Now I'm organizing and doing administration for the group." When I pointed out to her that her early working experiences were writing and organizing, she said she hadn't associated them.

Jacqui's daughter also writes for a newspaper, a small-town paper in the Midwest. Mothers like Jacqui often don't realize the influence they have had on their daughters. Because Jacqui's pay has been minimal and, at times, nonexistent, she does not take credit for what she has learned and accomplished. Often during our discussion she used the words *I fell into*—as if her employment were accidental—a phrase I never heard from daughters. She has taught language classes and now is studying the language of her latest refugee group. Her writing skills were honed under two fine editors. Her accomplishments merit praise, not self-effacement.

A mother may have taken a backseat to promote the skills and aspirations of husband or children, but when the last child leaves, she has the opportunity to shine. One daughter who is living at home for a few months told me that she and her mother have the same agenda. They both want to find new opportunities. She laughed and said, "I'm 24, and we both want the same thing."

Daughters speak with pride about their mothers' changes and achievements in their midlife. But not all mothers can or do take advantage of this newer, freer stage of life.

Unfulfilled Dreams

"The thing that concerns me about my generation," a 54-year-old businesswoman told me, "is the number of women that I see who really seem very unfulfilled or who seem to be a little bit lost. I just keep thinking this is an issue that will right itself in a lot of ways because the next generation will be more likely to have focused careers, and I think that will be part of the solution."

When a daughter enters her twenties, her single-life experience, some mothers are at a loss. The midlife years can generate feelings of self-pity and rejection. Those mothers may demand attention and not appreciate the fact that their daughters need time for themselves. Even though daughters can attempt to fill their mothers' loneliness, they cannot and should not be expected to fulfill their mothers' hopes. "When my daughter leaves, I think I may have to go into therapy," moaned a mother whose youngest daughter was graduating from college, "because I'm going to be living alone with an alcoholic [her husband]."

A sense of immobilization that sometimes overcomes mothers is felt also by daughters. The advice that a 23-year-old gave to herself as she entered the job market is good advice for mothers. "Sometimes I think you can be paralyzed in your head, and you do it with your legs."

When Natalie's husband announced to her that he no longer loved her and had found another woman, Natalie was overwhelmed with grief. Unaware that her husband of twenty-eight years had been seeing this "other woman," she was completely unprepared for his departure. Now, left with a home to sell which will be a major part of her settlement, she strives to connect to something. Her daughters cannot provide the support she needs and wants desperately. She is desolate. When she occasionally pulls herself out of her despondency, she can function. But on most days, she feels as though she is in limbo. Any plans she had to follow her flights of fancy during midlife have evaporated.

"When people are unable to move from disconnection to connection, the resulting combination of immobilization and isolation may become a prison," writes researcher Judith V. Jordan.[5] Some women enter that prison. They cannot connect with others.

Women who find themselves alone in midlife, because of divorce or death of a spouse, may feel overwhelmed by that constant reminder of their aloneness—the daughter's empty room. Filling the void with a new job or a commitment to a worthy cause may not be easy. When their daughters are single and grandchildren are not in the picture, they can be at a complete loss. They long for their daughters to take up the slack in their lives, to become their confidantes, their comforters. Then daughters are torn between their own needs to establish their own homes and friends and the needs of their mothers.

If these mothers could reach out to others, they would find

both release and energy. But mothers who were raised in a pre-talk-show, tell-it-all environment may find asking for help too difficult. Experts in stress management used to advise clients, particularly women, to toughen up and get control of the situation—no sharing of their distress.

Now therapists realize that acknowledging a need for support is more effective than projecting a stiff upper lip. Good friends help each other by offering and receiving consolation and advice. Through this give-and-take, women learn which relationships to trust: which are mutual, and which are controlling. Then they are better able to move beyond the "isolation" that accompanies stress, "whether this is a relationship with another person, feeling part of nature, or some aspect of spiritual involvement. It is when we feel the most separate from others and from the flow of life that we are most at risk," writes Jordan. Jordan calls this ability to go beyond isolation, *relational resilience.*[6]

Midlife mothers need that resiliency. Some contemplate divorce or remarriage. Many mothers' dreams of spending their lives with men they loved will not be fulfilled. One woman, recently divorced, regretted she would not "grow old with the man she had grown up with." Their shared experiences of struggling through the early years of marriage, surviving the "seven-year itch," and raising children would not be part of their midlife years. Many spouses, fathers or mothers, plan their departure from home to coincide with the departure of their children so the daily routines of caring for others and enjoying family are altered permanently. Women, truly alone for the first time, know they have to reach out to friends. Their daughters may offer comfort, but they have their own lives to lead. Mothers need confidantes of the same age, and so do daughters.

Reality

Once mothers grasp the reality of separation and realize that their daughters are capable young women, able to make their own decisions, they settle into their postchildren years. Mothers and daughters develop a new relationship and enter into some of their most rewarding years together. They are women in transition, looking forward to exploring new phases of their lives and getting to know each other as adults.

3

Searching for Connections
Through Friends

While I was lingering over a book on friendship at my local bookstore, a saleswoman, noticing my interest, volunteered a story about her sister. Her sister never had a "girlfriend," and now that she is getting divorced she realizes how much she needs a confidante. Although the saleswoman felt sorry for her sister, especially since their mother disapproves of the divorce, she thinks her sister should have thought about friends sooner. She herself has a friend she's known since age 12. She cherishes their friendship and feels "guilty" that her sister doesn't have a similar bond.

The theme of friendship resonates with all women and emerged again and again in my discussions with mothers and daughters—their desire, their need for, and their reliance on good, close friends. Mothers and daughters depend on women friends for laughter, advice, sympathy, companionship, and love. Although mothers' and daughters' reliance on friends is equally intense, their friendships reflect the uniqueness of their generations.

Daughters grew up knowing that they would share apartments with friends and marry late, so their "girlfriends" form an essential core of their young-adult lives. Now in the ranks of single, employed women, they continually expand their network of friends, meeting new friends through old friends and through coworkers.

Their mothers, because they married early, formed their closest circle of friends as a couple; through their children or through their work, but as a couple. They kept in touch with their earlier friends, but their "nights out" were spent with other mothers and fathers, only occasionally with girlfriends. Now, without children at home, mothers are reaching out to old friends or searching for new friends who want to spend time with them, not because of their husband or children but because of themselves.

Daughters

The "We" Generation

"I like to think of myself and my friends as part of the 'we' generation," Marta, age 24, said. Surprised to hear the word *we*, I asked her what she meant. "When a problem arises, we think about how we can fix it. We just don't let it go and wait for someone else to fix it. My friends say, 'This is how I learned how to handle this, and I'll help you if you want me to.' "

Marta explained a characteristic of daughters that I observed frequently during my interviews: Young women help one another "fix it." Her expression of solidarity with women of her generation particularly impressed me because Marta and other twenty-somethings were preceded by the "me" generation. Labeled "me" because of their self-absorption, that generation was known for competing with each other to make more money, build bigger homes, and raise smarter children. I marveled that a transformation in attitude and behavior could happen so quickly. Because Marta radiated a generosity of spirit, I wondered at first if her experience of support among colleagues and friends was unique. Did people help her because she is so willing to help them? Is she a throwback to the women of the fifties who were conditioned to set aside their own self-interests and put others—spouses, children, community—first? What characterizes the "we" generation?

Although Marta unquestionably is generous, she also is the woman who quit her first job because she was not respected by her bosses. She has not put aside her self-interests. To the contrary, she focuses on what she wants. One of her top priorities is to be part of a community of friends. She believes in working hard to form that community. She and her friends assume that they can cooperate with each other, work harmoniously with fellow employees, and achieve success.

Cooperation in the Workplace

This generation of women does not scorn or back away from competition but looks at competition in an impersonal way. The company (or other organization) may compete with other companies (or organizations), but within the corporate structure, people can cooperate with each other and still attain success. Many schools introduced "cooperative learning" into the elementary classroom when these women were young. They often sat around tables, discussed social problems, and felt at ease questioning their teachers. They may have competed for grades but did not like to compete against each other. They expect the same type of atmosphere in the workplace—work with each other, and everyone will benefit.

Janie, a 27-year-old who works in the film industry (known for its cutthroat attitude), commented on her age group within the business: "I don't think we're out to get each other. We all work well together and are friendly. We don't try to hide someone else's accomplishments to boost our own."

Her words define the basic meaning of *cooperation*, "the act of working or acting together or jointly for a common purpose or benefit."[1] Women's cooperative attitudes in the workplace have been noted by Deborah Tannen and other researchers, and may not be unique to this generation of women.[2] However, what I do think is unique is the expectation that cooperative behavior will lead to as many promotions and awards as competitive behavior. These women don't hide their dismay at colleagues who don't do their share of the work or who take credit for work they did not do. They speak up and expect fair play among all their working colleagues.

Networking at Work

One of the unique features of this generation is that they are finding female mentors in their careers, some of them becoming good friends. When I asked about role models, many mentioned the woman they presently worked for or a working woman who had given them a break. They found jobs through women friends, advanced with women bosses, and sought advice from women in their companies. Because of their acceptance in the workplace, the "we" generation almost spontaneously knows how to form a "new girl network."

"I never thought of going into the film business," Janie said. "But a friend of mine knew I was restless and looking for something. She was making a short film all on her own, no money, and I just started doing things for her movie and it was fun." Now Janie works with a major film studio, having learned her skills and found her jobs through a network of women friends. She and her friends discuss and berate the "old boy network" that operates in many industries, including theirs, but they are confident that their friends will be with them on their way up the corporate ladder. They see women ahead of them and know that each year the glass ceiling that used to prevent women from advancing in companies is being shattered. They are the right age at the right time.

Not everyone wants to climb the corporate ladder. The women who are not dedicated to a career freely admit that they don't want to work that hard. When I talked with Sue and Jen, who met while working in retail, Sue was determined to become a manager and make money while Jen admitted she did not want to work long hours with added responsibility. Jen laughed, attributing their attitudes to their place in the family. "Sue's the first in her family and always wants to be in control of everything, and I'm the youngest in my family and I always say, 'Okay, whatever you say.' " In their four months of working together, they discovered many mutual interests and learned to tolerate, even appreciate, each other's differences. I'm sure that when Sue becomes a manager, Jen will benefit from their network.

The "we" generation's collaborative attitude is evident in the workplace but is most pronounced in their personal lives, when they talk with friends.

The Living Room Analysts

Because of their mutual support, young women are replacing the psychiatrist's couch with their girlfriend's living room chair. The skills that therapists hone through years of listening to patients come almost intuitively to these women. I never heard them criticize a friend. I only heard efforts to understand and sympathize with each other. A 25-year-old who did not get the job she wanted (and was qualified for) acknowledges that the woman who secured the job was a better candidate. They are now friends. She is not atypical. This generation rejoices in friends' and acquaintances' accomplishments and empathizes with disappointments. Suggestions about jobs, family, and boyfriends are offered but only after listening carefully. Although they give each other advice, no one seems hurt if the advice is not followed—a true give-and-take between friends. I asked a group of women whom they would consult first if they were concerned about a relationship with a boyfriend. "I would go to my friends first," replied a woman while the others nodded in agreement. "My mom might freak out."

Friends are consulted first, understanding mothers next, and finally therapists. In some stress-filled urban settings, women flock to therapists and consider therapy part of their weekly routine. But most women in their twenties go directly to friends to find comfort and support. Not only can a good friend offer listening skills, she also senses when a friend should see a therapist. A wise friend realizes when problems need a professional approach. As Janie, the woman in the film industry, put it, "We're all trying to help each other."

The New Extended Family

Friendships have assumed added significance since most young women do not live with their parents and often live far away from siblings. The phenomenon of unmarried women living on their own is unique to the American and some other Western cultures. In many countries, young women are expected to remain with their families until they marry. Whether the marriage is arranged or the woman chooses her own mate, she will live at home with women relatives as her companions. But in the United States, a daughter wants to live on her own or with roommates who share her generational hopes and angst. Her roommates and friends form her support group, a self-selected extended family.

I spoke with clusters of young women whose support groups

ranged from friends from high-school days, classmates from college, "friends of friends" they met after graduation, and women from work. Their willingness to share stories, commiserate over mothers' comments, sympathize with slights from boyfriends, or vent frustrations about colleagues at work verifies the authenticity of research that suggests that a woman sees herself "in relation" to others. She learns and grows through her bonds of friendship.

The fact that these young women seek friends as a source of support does not mean they give up their individual lives or lose a sense of autonomy. They reflect the psychological literature that shows that women who have high levels of *individuation*— "the ability to function in an autonomous manner without being impaired or feeling overly responsible for significant others"— are able to find the support and connection they needs.[3] These findings are not news to women who know that seeing themselves "in relation" to others is a strength.

Our discussions centered on people, those they loved, those they felt sorry for, and those they avoided. They lamented their own shortcomings, acknowledged their talents, and clearly described their frustrations. Their goal is to connect with others, to deepen relationships, to be loved. Within the friend or work environment, they want to establish genuine community. They know that working together creates a synergy that can be more effective than a singular effort.

Because women are not marrying as young as they did in their mothers' time, they do not think of female friends as substitutes for boyfriends. They like spending evenings with girlfriends. Their mothers often considered a "date" a higher priority than a night with friends. When these women make plans to spend evenings or weekends together, the commitments are kept, not dropped if a man calls.

As their lives grow more complex with increasing work obligations, many women complain that they don't have enough time to nurture their friendships. They must work to maintain friends. But they are willing to put extra effort into a friendship and search for more time, just to talk and listen.

In *Gender and Discourse*, Deborah Tannen comments on conversations between two 25-year-old women who participated in her research: "The fact that [they] showed less discomfort finding a topic, elaborated topics at greater length, physically squirmed less and generally looked more physically relaxed, seems to indicate that they found it easier to fulfill the assigned task of sitting in a room and talking to each other than did the boys and men."[4]

I noticed the same ease, willingness, and comfort level that Tannen observed. Discourse between friends flows naturally. "I have a resource of girlfriends," a 26-year-old said. "We hash out everything. I'll get a phone call from someone who says, 'I just need to see you. Can we get together for coffee?' Even though I'm busy, I set time aside and go. I think my girlfriends are my touchstone because the generations are so different. I mean my mom just doesn't understand what my day is like." Girlfriends understand what it is like to be on your own, in a city, supporting yourself.

Not all daughters live far away. One woman who moved back with her family for six months before heading for a job in another state meets regularly with two friends who also are living at home temporarily. "We've all moved home, so we get together and complain together," she said. "We know what the other is going through. When I go to my friend's house and she's fighting with her parents, I can sympathize and tell her I fought with my parents about that too." Whether the problem is persuading parents to loosen up on behavioral expectations, trying to get a boyfriend to make a commitment, or finding the right job, the women share comparable experiences.

Young women's friendships are resilient and adjust to many transitions during the decade of the twenties. They change apartments, switch jobs, leave town, acquire boyfriends. Each shift brings a new element to the friendship. "I left to go to graduate school when I was 26," explained Aggie as she described the changes in her friendship patterns. "I returned at age 28, and everyone had coupled. Before we always got together with individual women. Now we get together with Susie and Steve and Jenny and Ben. At first that threw me for a loop because I didn't want to become a couple society where we didn't have any single friends. But that's not what happened." Aggie related how their group has managed to include boyfriends in their close network of friends. Friendship has become an art form, blending different people within a framework of location. The extended families of young, single adult women eventually include boyfriends and career friends.

Friends tell each other of job openings, find roommates for one another, and connect their girlfriends with boyfriends. Most of the time their kindness is appreciated, but sometimes they may find themselves left out. Twenty-nine-year old Jody laughed as she told me: "Recently I introduced two female friends and two male friends who started dating. All of a sudden I was the odd person out, and instead of having four friends, I had two couples I didn't see. It's much improved now because I basically told them that I'd take them back." She did not hesitate to remind her friends where they had met their boyfriends. Jody's honesty, humor, and willingness to confront good friends rather than brood over hurt feelings show she grasps the meaning of friendship.

These women understand each other's decision to delay marriage and pursue careers more than their mothers do. Although some women claim that their mothers are great friends—even their best friends—their network of same-age friends offers a generational bond that mothers cannot provide.

In a similar way, a daughter cannot supply her mother with the kind of friendship that a mother's same-age friend can. A daughter and mother may share a family history but they have not experienced the same generational happenings. All women need friends who have lived through events common to their generation.

Mothers

At twenty we find our friends for ourselves,
but it takes Heaven
to find us one when we are fifty-seven.

—W. H. Auden, *City Without Walls*[5]

Some mothers envy their daughters' ability to share experiences and deepest feelings with friends. Mothers who are in their middle to late fifties (or early sixties) were raised at the tail end of the "silent" generation (right before the baby boomers). They learned that their role precluded revealing inner thoughts, that others' feelings came first. Mothers who are in their late forties and early fifties probably received ambivalent messages about the value of their emotions. Many parroted other people or the latest "self-help" book rather than delving deeply into their own feelings. Both sets of mothers, therefore, admire a daughter's ability to remain aware of and sensitive to her own inner needs, while heeding the needs of her friends.

Some mothers, perhaps most mothers, cannot reveal themselves to groups of friends as quickly as their daughters can. Because of this reserve, they may find themselves emotionally restrained as they enter midlife. Their exterior may present contentment, but on the inside many yearn to discuss what they are feeling. They search for an intimate circle of friends with whom they can share the evolving emotions of midlife.

"A History of Friends"

"You have to have a history with friends to keep friends," commented Anita as she talked about the many changes in her life.
She, like many midlife women, has followed her husband to his
job locations, changed her job to accompany her husband,
adjusted to living in diverse communities, and made acquaintances in each new place. Close friends were hard to develop
because she kept moving. Anita attempted to meet people in
communities where friendship groups were formed long before
she arrived. She seldom called or visited her high-school or college friends and lost touch with friends from previous locations.
Now she regrets that she neglected old friends.

Anita is not unique in her quest or her regrets. Sometimes keeping track of old friends helps a woman keep her emotional balance. One executive told me that she telephones her
elementary-school friend once a week, and they talk for an hour.
Because of her busy schedule and family obligations, she can't
take time for personal lunches with new friends, so the phone
call to her longtime friend takes the edge off her lack of close
new friends.

For mothers in midlife, maintaining old friendships and
meeting new people present a challenge. A dear friend may
move because of a major change in an industry, or she (or her
husband) may take an "early retirement" and move to another
community.

Lorraine thought she had a friend that she could rely on forever. She considered herself fortunate to have a "nonkin confidante" who shared her worries about children, concerns about
work, and frustrations with life in a community that neither of
them particularly liked. But Lorraine's friend moved when her
husband was "retired" in a major downsizing of his company,
and Lorraine was devastated. "Her move was the hardest thing
I've had to deal with recently," she said, fighting back tears. "I

had lunch with her weekly, and we played tennis every Saturday. When she left in September, it was awful. It was like a death, and I couldn't believe it. It's still horrible. I thought I was going to die. I confided everything in her. We had known each other for years."

Women friends offer each other an empathy, a sensitivity to issues that family members may not realize are important. A mother may display a strength that cloaks her true feelings of sorrow or inadequacy. She may not tell anyone some of her deepest secrets.

Because of the anonymity of our interviews, some women spoke of events that they had concealed from family and friends. Some referred to incidents of childhood or teenage sexual abuse that they are too embarrassed to mention to family. Others quietly spoke of struggles to have abortions when abortions were banned in the United States. To disclose a heart-aching story requires a history of rapport and trust with a friend. This bond takes time to develop, and often women do not remain in their communities long enough to develop the bond, or the bond is too fragile, based on snatches of conversation amid social settings. Because mothers are less comfortable than their daughters in revealing themselves to friends, they may turn more readily to a therapist during a crisis. They don't want to burden their friends or don't believe their friends would be willing to listen.

They also desire to meet new friends. "This is the age," Lorraine said, "when a lot of people we know are in transition. Kids are finished [with] college. I look around and realize that I work all day. I'm not making new friends. I'm not meeting anyone. I belong to some organizations, and I see people at meetings and chitchat, but I'm not making friends. I don't have the time." Lorraine and her friend who moved away telephone each other regularly, and Lorraine plans to visit her soon. But she realizes she needs a close friend, one who lives nearby, and finds it difficult at midlife to make the transition.

Some communities ease the process of making friends by offering a myriad of activities for women, while other communities are less sensitive to their residents' needs. Even people who live in close proximity, in apartment buildings or town houses, may encounter indifference when they attempt to engage neighbors in conversation.

Sally, for instance, regrets that she ever moved into the suburb where she currently lives. She found it easier to make friends in her old community. "In the Newcomers' Club in this town, people always complain that it's very hard to make friends," she said. "People here just don't take the extra move. They're nice, but you don't see them again. I've made one friend since I've moved here, and we meet every month for dinner."

"And when you don't have children, you don't have an entrée," reported another woman in the group. Every woman in the room agreed. "Children provide the entrée, and I'm tired of the 32-year-olds in our Newcomers' Club with their two-year-old babies. I've been there and done that." And then she added, "It takes a long time to really have a friend, but it's easy to have acquaintances."

A mother's friends usually came through activities that were related to child rearing. She made plans with other mothers of same-age children and worked hard to keep up the friendships with women whose children did not attend the same schools. If she worked outside the home, the demands of family usually required that she come home right after work. Her work friends were seen during office hours only. But now without children, she can spend more time with her friends from work.

"During the school year," said a school administrator, "two women I work with are my best friends, and we talk about everything. I lose touch with my other friends, and it's difficult to call someone up in the summer and say, 'Let's have lunch.' So I don't call because I think they're too busy. They have their own lives, or they have other friends. I should be making more of an effort, but I'm too tired."

Missing Out

Many mothers I interviewed felt they were missing out, missing out on sharing their lives with a close friend—a same-age woman, a nonkin confidante—someone who has experienced what they have, not only in family life but in the events of their generation. Their mothers and their daughters may provide friendship, but they belong to other generations, not theirs. Wars, economic downswings, the women's movement affect each generation, but in different ways. Women of similar age can recall milestones that shaped their lives as women.

When I asked two women, who met for the first time during our interview in a suburb of Washington, D.C., to tell me about their friends, they responded in very similar terms. "I don't have any friends," replied Vickie, a very attractive 49-year-old woman. She teaches in a small college-prep private school that has a very young faculty. Because boundaries are clearly established between teachers and parents, the mothers of students in the school have not attempted to draw her into their social activities. Vickie is treated as an employee, not as a potential friend. "I look to my dear friend who lives in Tennessee to sustain my mental health," she said. "We have so much in common. I can get on the phone with her for an hour and a half, two hours, without knowing the time had past."

The other woman, Rosemary, replied to my question about friends by saying, "It's knocking me out." She laughed and explained what she meant: "How do you make friends? I know friendships are made through commonality. I would love to join a women's group at my church, but they meet at nine in the morning so I'm excluded because I work on the day it is scheduled. I'm knocking myself out trying to figure out how to make friends."

Rosemary told me that a friend of hers (whom she thought had many friends) commented that she was glad they had met because Rosemary was her only friend. Rosemary thought to herself, "If she's having a problem with friends, imagine the problem I have." Those who feel they are "missing out" must reach out to others, and that requires effort and, perhaps, a rethinking of interests and priorities. To make and keep friends requires work.

New Interests

When women branch out in midlife to pursue new interests or new jobs, they have to work to maintain old friends who may not feel the need to develop further interests. One woman who became fascinated with the interplay of international politics and religion found that she had a hard time keeping her favorite subject out of her conversations. Her friends weren't the least bit interested in her research and study. She didn't want to seem impolite, but she now found her old friends rather boring and was looking for new groups to join. She found like-minded people in a foreign-relations study course.

Joan Borysenko, writing about women's lives, advises, "As the ovaries begin to make less estrogen and more androgens [male hormones] we figuratively develop the hormonal balls to set our boundaries and decline invitations that do not feel nourishing."[6] Finding the strength to say no to an invitation, even if women have developed the "hormonal balls," is not always easy. Women want to expand, not limit, their circle of friends. But a woman who finds that a friend drains her energy would do well to reevaluate the relationship and strive to meet women who bring her nourishment and vitality.

I asked a particularly gregarious woman who had recently

been hired as a manager of an art gallery how she planned to meet people with whom she could share her interests. After a pause, she confessed she didn't know how to reach out. "Volunteer activity, even in the arts, seems so superficial," she said. "We get together and talk about a project and move on. There's no deep bonding, and it's a frustration, a loss. We change so dramatically at this age. We begin questioning and thinking and are almost afraid to mention it to other people. I want that deeper connection, and the other stuff doesn't seem as much fun as when I was in my thirties and early forties. I want to say, 'Don't just gossip to me. Let's talk about real things.' That's how I feel exactly, and that means moving out to other people or on a different level with the same people." She is still searching.

When Priscilla returned to graduate school after being a full-time mom and part-time volunteer in her community, she quickly discovered she had to limit her community activities if she was going to be a serious student and plan for a midlife career. Although some of her friends understood her need to drop her regular commitments, others seemed to resent her determination to begin a career. When I spoke with her, she told me about her practice in alternative-type physical therapy and her speaking engagements to groups that are exploring the body-mind connections. Now most of her friends, she said, are colleagues in her field, but she relies on one or two old friends who shared her restlessness. They themselves have developed fuller lives in midlife. They are each other's confidantes. She no longer sees those friends she encountered only through sports or volunteer work.

Fear of Disconnection

In a neighboring town, a very popular woman, active in community organizations, killed herself. She was a woman that "everyone knew." "She always looked so great," a friend of hers told me. "I called several people who knew her well and asked, 'How could this happen?' Nobody knew the depth of her anguish. No one understood." As I reflected with her on her friend's death, she wondered, "Are we so scattered that everyone looks at everyone else and thinks they're doing well? We don't know that other people are feeling alone, feeling alienated. I think women once they're in their fifties need a community to talk about deeper things together."

Would a community have helped this woman? Was she in therapy? No one seems to know the answer. The loss of connection, family, or friends, can create an overwhelming sense of despair. Some women feel that despair when their children leave home. Many therapists now suggest that their clients join self-help groups, groups that help women understand that they are not alone—that others also are lonely. Joining a group of sympathetic women may be a first step in conquering the voices of self-doubt and emptiness.

However, not all support groups offer the guidance that women need. Support groups and community activities can provide a path to wholeness and energy, but just "joining and doing," as Beth described her frantic search for connection, can't fulfill a woman's need. The many organizations and self-awareness groups that Beth joined led her to "a false set of connections and a false sense of security." Beth was right to explore the opportunities in her community, but she should have narrowed her interests and concentrated on one or two groups or organizations that she could investigate in depth. An in-depth exploration may provide the "entrée" to friendships that was lost when her children grew up.

Longtime Friends

Not all women feel the need to reach out for new confidantes. Longtime friends can be equally as stimulating as new friends as they share with each other their midlife explorations. Just as a woman and her spouse can change through the years and enjoy their transformations through various stages of life, so can women.

Bunny and her friends have known each other since their children were in elementary school together. When I interviewed them, they laughed over their common experiences (like agonizing over their daughters' boyfriends) and commiserated over their serious problems (like dealing with one husband's unexpected demand for divorce and another husband's depression). Each of these women has worked or actively volunteered since their children entered school, so they also bring work and community experiences into their conversations. They are comfortable with themselves and each other. Although they were anxious about a number of issues, friendship was not one of them. "I feel I've been very fortunate to have an amazing community of friends," said one of the group. "They are people who are just interesting and into so many things, and they've opened up lots of different doors." "I've had many years of fabulous friends," said another. "That's the best gift we have. Loneliness is the biggest issue with many people."

I observed that at times they could finish each other's sentences or interrupt with their own perception of the event we were discussing. Deborah Tannen calls this *cooperative overlap*. Tannen's analysis of a Thanksgiving dinner in which everyone interrupted everyone else made clear to her that some speakers "consider talking along with another to be a show of enthusiastic participation in the conversation, of solidarity, of creating connections."[7] Others may consider the overlap only impolite. However, Tannen noted that if speakers equally overlap each other, symmetry exists, not domination. Within this group of animated fifty-something women, no one dominated.

In another group of equally accomplished and dynamic women friends, I observed very little interruption or "overlap." These women listened intently and waited quietly when one or the other paused to think through an episode or to collect her emotions. I loved seeing the difference between these two groups of longtime friends. Both groups understood each other's style of communicating, and each showed respect and listened, but in entirely different ways. The experience helped me understand (and I will discuss this in chapter four) how individual pairs of mothers and daughters may have to find the right comfort zone that will bring forth the best communication.

Maintaining Friends

At some point mothers and daughters realize that friends need maintenance. One day in the midst of writing about adolescents, I realized that I needed contact with real, live adult women, instead of the computer and adolescents. As much as I loved talking with adolescents and writing about them, I hungered for conversations with women my own age. But I didn't have enough free time to arrange for a lunch or dinner meeting. So I made a pact with myself that at least once a week I would telephone a woman whom I had not seen for a while and catch up with what was happening in her life. Although the lives of the women I called were as busy as mine and I respected that, talking with them made me feel wonderful. Even if a phone call is the only contact possible, the connection needs to be made.

In her book *Friendshifts: The Power of Friendship and How It Shapes Our Lives*, Jan Yager recommends ways to make and keep friends.[8] The following are some of her suggestions that can be adopted by both mothers and daughters.

"Be likable" heads her list. Certainly most will agree that a person who complains constantly or never smiles will not make or keep friends easily.

"Be concerned with your friend" speaks for itself and is the basis for friendship. If a friendship is based on an insincere motive (such as getting into the right circle or climbing the social or business ladder), the concern will not be genuine. That friend should be dropped.

"Be positive and upbeat" is a suggestion that is not always easy for friends to follow. Friends should be there for each other when either one is feeling lousy, negative, and downbeat. A person with a positive and upbeat attitude can make a dreary day brighter and is needed when nothing seems right.

"Avoid misusing friends as therapists or bankers"—good advice in general but not in all cases. Most young women talk with friends as openly as they would talk with a therapist and benefit from their exchange. However, a good friend quickly recommends a therapist if she discovers that the problem is deep-rooted or if she is overwhelmed by her friend's anguish. Also, on rare occasions loans can be successful. One woman I interviewed loaned her friend a substantial amount for a partial down payment on a house. Since the borrower was a new physician and the lender an established physician, the lender was confident that the money would be repaid, and it was. That type of friendly transaction does not always work, but keep in mind that sometimes it does.

"Listen carefully with empathy"—amen.

"Keep a friendship as comfortable as possible, taking your cues from your friend's needs and abilities." This suggestion applies particularly with women who are balancing busy lives. If a friendship becomes too demanding on one party, the other party isn't giving enough consideration to the concerns of her friend. Everyone has her pace, and good friends walk, talk, work in sync.

"Keep confidences." Trustworthiness is a top requirement of good friends. This advice also applies to mothers and daughters when they confide in each other. A trustworthy friend is loved.

"Share your knowledge and experiences with your friends." Good conversations stem from sharing knowledge and experience, and the art of friendship includes good conversation.

Women know that good friends are worth thinking about, and Yager's suggestions will help stimulate thought.

Women's Movement: Women Friends

I recall the first time I was fully exposed to the "women's movement." I was attending a meeting held at the Aspen Institute during the sixties, and a professor from a Midwestern college spoke about the "feminine mystique" (her talk was based on Betty Friedan's book). I, like many in my generation, had been raised in an environment in which men were considered far more interesting, bright, and companionable than women. The professor's presentation and my subsequent conversations with her and her woman companion raised my awareness of my own attitudes toward men and women. Realizing what a disservice I had done to myself and my friends (our daughters were not yet born), I returned home to the small Midwestern town I was living in at the time, determined to learn all I could about feminism. My personal search to honor myself through knowing more about women channeled my interests and subsequent career in a new direction.

I asked many mothers if they were affected by the women's movement, and, to my surprise, most did not credit feminism for raising their sights for themselves. They talked more about how feminism had affected their daughters' decisions about career and marriage. Mothers who themselves were engaged in careers tended to think of their employment in terms of individual opportunities, not a national movement. Their dynamism in midlife sprang from their need to be productive and useful. However, in my observation, feminism sensitized all women to their place in the social, economic, and political fabric of the country. The movement has reached inside every home and touched both mothers and daughters.

Now a generation of young-adult daughters takes for granted that women are entitled to the same opportunities and rights as men and do not doubt that their opinions are just as valid as men's. Their affection and support for each other stems from an unfiltered view of themselves as every bit as engaging and capable as their male friends. They bond with each other without a sense of rivalry and trust each other as true friends. They are the "we" generation. The anxiety they feel does not come from pressure from friends; it comes from pressures they place on themselves as they ponder their many options. Friends are there to help them. And as their mothers are released from family obligations, they discover that friends can be there for them, too.

4

Communicating
with Each Other

Reaching Out

"She was totally uncommunicative for five years," Ana said as she described her daughter, Sara. "She wanted nothing to do with us." During high school, Sara acted as though she could not stand her mother. She talked back to the point that Ana at last told her to leave, that she had "had it." Sara lived with a friend's family for a month before she agreed to come home. The agitation between Ana and Sara lasted until Sara's freshman year in college, when she telephoned her mother and said, "I miss you. I need you." Ana wept as she spoke of her daughter's turnaround. "When she came home, she was like another person. She actually sat down and talked with us. She didn't go upstairs and close the door. She joined us for meals, went out for dinner with us."

Did Sara's transformation come about because she was leaving adolescence behind, or was it the result of her mother and father's unrelenting determination not to lose their daughter? It was the combination of both. Her maturity and her parents' commitment convinced Sara to embrace her family once again.

The adolescent testing of parents and a daughter's overwhelming fear of becoming her mother usually end after high school. A daughter wanting to differentiate herself from her mother may have blocked any true communication between them. However, as she matures and sees her family in a new light, often helped by the college experience of living with roommates from many types of families, she develops a new appreciation of her parents.

Many Ways of Communicating

Not all daughters are "totally uncommunicative" during high school. Some actually converse with their mothers. Even daughters within the same family aren't necessarily alike. Ana's older daughter, Jan, never distanced herself from her parents. Ana recalled that Jan loved to chat and told her "almost everything" during high school. The same familiarity continued through Jan's college years. She and her mother talked regularly, discussing classes, boyfriends, girlfriends.

When Ana was talking about her two completely different daughters, I was reminded of the research that surveyed 35,000 parents, asking at what age they could characterize their children on a scale from very strong-willed to very compliant. The survey revealed that most parents can describe their children's distinctive personalities shortly after birth.[1] Mothers often comment on the uniqueness of each child. When a mother is aware of a daughter's particular temperament, she may find that she has to communicate in different ways, especially if her daughter does not have her personality. In Ana's family, for instance, one daughter was more open and sharing, while the other needed time to find a confirmation of herself before she could open up—a challenge for parents who want a cohesive family.

A more typical mother-daughter pair is Susan and her daughter. They never were hostile to each other during her high-school years, but they had many moments of disagreement, some major. But now Susan notices the changes in her 21-year-old daughter. "She has come out of that awful part when daughters don't believe anything you say," Susan said. "Now if I say, 'What a beautiful day,' she'll agree instead of saying, 'Yesterday was prettier.' We really have so many things in common now. We look forward to seeing each other. She's such a nice person. I'm thrilled."

Those without daughters may find it strange to hear a mother rejoice in her discovery that her 21-year-old daughter is "nice." What mothers typically interpret as "not nice" is a daughter's firm rejection of her mother's inclination to mold and shape her. After high school, when a daughter no longer lives at home full-time, a mother is more relaxed. The result is a daughter who is less wary about control issues and who is willing to converse.

As I interviewed mothers and daughters, I marveled at the many ways they communicate with each other. Some call or E-mail each other daily, others talk once or twice a week, and some less frequently. The number of contacts does not necessarily indicate the depth of the connection.

Mothers reflect their own personalities when they talk with their young-adult daughters. A few are comfortable sharing their inner thoughts, but most, accustomed to being the listener, feel uncomfortable. "I don't let her, I don't let anyone, know the times I haven't felt so confident and secure," the mother of a 27-year-old confessed. "Maybe I should have expressed that more often. I have always felt that I have to be strong, but I'm working on opening up."

As mothers begin to open up in midlife, so do their daughters. "I'm not afraid of being disliked," said a mother who experienced tumultuous adolescent years with her daughter (now 22), "and she's not afraid of being rejected. We can be more forthright with each other."

Once daughters feel more secure and good about themselves and more accepting of their mothers, an adult-to-adult conversation can begin. Betty, whose daughter is a chef, said that "even though I've been in the food business for years, I now defer to her in the kitchen. It's wonderful—we call and exchange recipes." Mother and daughter have moved into a new stage.

Mother-Talk

Maura laughed as she described the progression of her contacts with her daughter. "When she was a sophomore, she called every Sunday at five—in junior year maybe every other Sunday. In senior year I was leaving messages all over the campus trying to get her to call me. There's a continuum of separation that's so appropriate." Now her daughter is living on the opposite coast, and they talk more frequently, sometimes daily through their E-mail. Their conversations vary from informational exchanges to emotional discussions.

As a daughter moves into her twenties, she views her mother more as an ally than an adversary. Because they usually do not live together, the phone calls or E-mails tend to be conversations about their lives rather than admonitions about safety or boyfriends or the college "service requests" (can you send me . . . ?). Mothers and daughters now are more likely to telephone just to talk. And talking is what mothers love to do with their daughters. "I make a point of chatting," Lillian told me. "My daughter now lives in Atlanta, and we talk every day about anything. I've never been a chatterer, but I am now because I want to keep a connection with her."

Types of Relationships

In a small study that looked at types of mother-daughter relationships, a University of Illinois researcher defined five kinds of mother-daughter relationships:

1. *Avoiders*. Both mother and daughter have ambivalent feelings toward each other and establish a pattern of distancing and reuniting.
2. *Caretakers*. The two parties have reversed roles to vulnerable mother and competent daughter.
3. *Repairers*. Mother and daughter exhibit tolerance and forgiveness and have moved from conflict to acceptance.
4. *Negotiators*. Both parties seek compromise and approval because a pattern of mutuality and approval-seeking has been established.
5. *Good friends*. Mother and daughter enjoy reciprocal feelings and have a continuous good relationship.[2]

Most of the women in the study had the last three types of relationships, as did the mothers and daughters whom I interviewed. They were repairers, negotiators, and good friends. Most, not all, had passed through the volatile stages of distancing and reuniting (characteristic of the avoiders), and a few were caretakers because of parental depression or parental financial needs.

Six Mothers, Six Styles

Seated around a large coffee table filled with art books in a roomy Washington apartment, six women in their early and middle fifties talked about their daughters. (The daughters were all single and ranged in age from 23 to 30.) None of the women knew each other well but had met through a mutual friend who asked them to come together for an interview. After they had conversed for a while and realized that their daughters had good jobs and were, according to their mothers, very bright, one mother said, "I'm totally convinced that our daughters come with something special, and our job is not to ruin it but to help them move forward with it. Maybe we're six women who did not interfere with that specialness."

Not only did these mothers not interfere with their daughters' "specialness," they have expressed their own specialness. Each started work at various times and for various reasons. The doctor has worked since she earned her medical degree; the lawyer went to law school when her children were school age; the therapist prepared for a career after her children were grown; the teacher returned to the classroom when her children were in middle school; the insurance rep gave up a career in advertising to stay home with her children and reentered business part-time when they were in school; the business owner started her own retail business when her children were in school. Five of the women are married, three to their "original" husbands and fathers of their daughters; two divorced women have remarried, and one remains single.

Their contacts with their daughters reflect their own personalities, their lifestyles, their desires for their daughters.

"Judy's the most independent young woman I've ever met," Fran said, describing her 24-year-old daughter. "She's been all over the world for her job. She's accomplished more than I ever knew someone at that age could." Although Judy is "independent," she and her mother talk five to ten times a week, thanks to Fran's toll-free business number. Although they talk freely about their everyday lives, Fran knows there is an "intimacy level about boyfriends that I feel is none of my business, and I'm quiet about it. Once in a while I'll be yearning to ask a question, but I don't." Fran later admitted that although she lets Judy set the boundaries on their conversations, she tries to give her some "semi-intimate" information because "I want to set that tone. I try to make sure I reveal something, like saying someone is driving me crazy at work or your dad and I really got into an issue." By showing her vulnerability, Fran is hoping her daughter may at some point reciprocate.

But they talk mostly about Judy's job and activities. "I like to chitchat with Judy, just as I would with a friend. That's goal number one for me." Fran acknowledges that "chitchatting" is not the goal of her husband and daughter but says, "He's fine and she's fine, and they have this great relationship."

By recognizing that she and her husband can have successful yet different styles of conversing with their daughter, Fran has encouraged Judy to enjoy each of them freely and fully. Judy talks with her dad in their own way (mostly about nonpersonal matters), and her mother does not feel left out.

Carol and her 29-year-old daughter, Betsy, both love reading and writing. Although they live in different parts of the country, they speak frequently, and Carol is very conscious of what she can and cannot say to her daughter. For instance, it took Carol four years to ask Betsy about her living status with her boyfriend. "I didn't ask," Carol said, "because I figure if she wants to tell me she will. Although we're quite close, there is a boundary. I'm aware of not impinging on a certain level, not putting her into an uncomfortable position, or I would not have taken four years to ask about him." Carol also did not want to be perceived as critical.

Aggie, on the other hand, talks with her daughters about everything, and her daughters reciprocate. "[They] tell me stuff I would never tell my mother," she said. But they weren't always this close. "My daughters didn't tell me everything when they were young because I would have gone ballistic. My daughter had an abortion when she was 18, and I'm sorry she didn't feel she could tell me at the time. Thank God it was an era that she could go someplace and it was safe. It was the right decision for her at age 18." That painful experience made Aggie more conscious of the need to remain open to her daughter. She believes that in moments of deep despair, a daughter should be able to reveal her anguish to her mother. Aggie learned the hard way and now makes a point to be a nonjudgmental listener and offers advice only when asked.

Katherine seemed surprised that some of the women in the room withheld comments to their daughters because they did not want to appear critical. Katherine raised her daughters by herself, feels very close to them, and offers them advice on all subjects. "My daughter [age 28] called and was telling me about a work situation," Katherine said. "I told her not to get caught up in it." She told her daughter, "Remember your values. If someone tells you to do something and you know it's not helpful or that it's immoral or criminal, why would you do it?"

Even though Katherine's daughters know they don't have to follow her advice, that they can "take it or leave it," she offers it anyway. She believes that this directness has paid off. Katherine has a genuine ease with her daughters, and they do not seem to resent her candor.

Silvia, because of her training as a therapist, is very conscious of the similarities and differences between her and her daughter, Barrie. She admires their differences and acknowledges that she would have been uncomfortable at Barrie's age (25) doing what she does—going to corporate dinners, sitting at the chairman's table, and traveling for business. But she worries about some similarities, especially as they relate to men. Silvia, now happily married, left Barrie's father when Barrie was one. She talks openly to Barrie about how she felt trapped in that marriage. But now she sees Barrie getting into issues with her dad (issues like women's role and sexuality) that she got into with him as a wife. That concerns her. "I have tried to talk to her about how to deal with that, but I don't think she always deals with him effectively," she said. "I worry about who she'll choose as a mate. I don't philosophize to her, but I tell her about my experience. Then she sees her dad and stepmother, who are very traditional, so I think she's seen both ways of living and she'll have to make her own choice."

The fear of "who she'll choose as a mate" rings through most mothers' discussions about daughters. Even though their daughters are achieving, competent, and productive, they still want to see their daughters happily married. Both divorced and married mothers know the importance of that decision. When they talk with their daughters, the subject of boyfriends or whether they are dating is not far from their minds. But they often avoid the subject, and their main conversations center on their jobs and everyday life.

Dottie's daughter is in medical school, following in a family tradition. She and her daughter live in the same town, work out together in the gym, and thoroughly enjoy each other's company. She expects great accomplishments from her daughter and doesn't hold back: "I told her that her father and I have developed a baseline which is very high, but that doesn't mean we want her to stay at that baseline; she has to achieve more." I asked how her daughter reacts to these high expectations. "She doesn't object to it," she replied. "She's happy that she has more than what my husband and I started out with. She—and her friends—are in a position to help others, and in helping others they will find self-satisfaction."

Dottie also hopes her daughter will find a good husband. Her daughter, mindful of her mother's wishes, will often telephone her at the hospital and asked her to come over for dinner, not revealing that a boyfriend will also be there. "I'll go to her apartment, looking ragged and worn out, not realizing that I'm going to meet someone who is very important, so I told her, 'Next time you want me to meet someone, warn me.' "

The bottom line with these mothers is their strong desire to keep in touch with their daughters, to know what is happening in their daughters' lives, to impart their wisdom. Most of them have accepted their daughters' lifestyle, their present single status, their desire to live alone or with friends. They may worry about their daughters' choice of mate, but they try hard not to bring up the subject too frequently.

When Talking Is Not So Easy

Even when their daughters are adults, some mothers never lose their desire to change or to mold them. This is especially true when mothers and daughters have different temperaments, their moments of affection do not coincide, and their troublesome relationship did not end after the high-school years. In such cases, it's more difficult for mothers to unconditionally love their daughters. A mother who struggled through her daughter's at-home years said, "You need a special grace to be able to give that unconditional love." Her daughter caused her many a sleepless night. Now she is living on her own, and her mother, reminding herself that her daughter is a 26-year-old woman, struggles to appreciate all her good qualities. But at times it's hard. Little things get in the way. "She picked me up at the airport with a big grin," she recalled. "And inside I'm saying, 'I wish she would wear lipstick. She's so beautiful.' Then I realize that what I'm saying is crazy— what a jerk I am even to think that way, but I do."

I'm sure her inner thoughts sound familiar to many mothers. (Another woman was embarrassed to walk with her 28-year-old daughter, who wore her long blonde hair in dreadlocks.) A mother wants everyone to appreciate her daughter's beauty, to acknowledge her insights, to love her. Yet accepting a daughter's lifestyle, clothing style, choice of job, or current boyfriend is not always easy. Mothers sometimes think they know what is best for their daughters, and the urge to direct them is hard to relinquish.

Most mothers at times make offhand remarks that can be interpreted by their daughters as criticism. If those comments are not immediately challenged and discussed, hurt feelings and misunderstandings soon follow. Rebecca and her daughter have reached a point in their relationship where if one of them (particularly Rebecca) says something that is perceived as critical, they clear the air quickly. Rebecca's daughter now will tell her mother when a comment was hurtful. Even though a remark was not intended to be critical, Rebecca apologizes for the hurt and they discuss what happened. Misunderstandings can happen in any close relationship. Without this clearing of the air, resentments build and end up damaging the relationship.

Many mothers have trouble not being judgmental. Because they come from a different generation, their views of the world are not the same as their daughters'. A mother may have a preconceived idea of how her daughter should be living, but her daughter has her own generational mind-set.

Silvia overcame her tendency to criticize her daughter's lifestyle. "I've learned not to be judgmental but to be curious," she said. "That's the best thing to do in any relationship. The more curious you are, the more you find out; and then you won't be judgmental anymore because you'll understand where she is coming from."

Silvia offers a perfect formula for communicating with a daughter.

Daughter-Talk

I was impressed that most young women have such a deep understanding of their mothers. Now, though not earlier, they can understand why their mothers were not always home, why they seemed preoccupied at times, why everything was not always perfect, why they and their mothers could not agree during adolescence. Daughters accept their mothers and, in many cases, really like them.

Giving Her What She Wants

Some mothers still demand too much, and their expectations interfere with good communications. But older daughters are more willing to tolerate their idiosyncrasies.

"I couldn't give my mother what she wanted," said Heather, a 30-year-old wilderness guide. "She wanted me to be her best friend. Now my sister-in-law is her best friend, and they do everything together." Because of her sister-in-law's closeness to her mother, Heather no longer shoulders the burden of being her mother's companion. She noted her mother even seems proud of her adventures: "She likes to tell her friends what I'm doing." Heather leads an unpredictable life. She works as a guide for short intervals to make money to travel on her own. "I don't have career plans. I just have plans—like going to Africa, biking through South America." She could not and did not want to give her mother the intimacy she craved. Thankfully, her brother's marriage solved their problem.

Heather wears a certain earring all the time, one given her by her mother. "It's the first thing that my mother ever gave me that I liked," she said quietly. "We have very different tastes." Heather never takes the earring off, not even during the night. When I asked her if she ever told her mother that she wears the earring all the time, she said she has not. Although Heather still is wary about her mother's need for closeness, she has developed a new appreciation of her and continually mentioned that her mother is supportive of her unconventional life.

Throughout our conversations, daughters were mindful of their mothers' generational differences. Often they excuse their mothers' anxiety about them because they realize their anxiousness stems from experience. Their mothers do not want their daughters to fall into the same pitfalls they did.

Lil's mother wants her daughter to have a career to "fall back on after children are raised" and is urging her to go to graduate school. Lil is torn between her own ambitions, which would not involve another degree, and her mother's. "She always says do this before you get married, so there is that tension between us," Lil said. "Is this what I want for myself right now, or is this what my mother wants for me?" Lil understands her mother's "pragmatic approach" to life, respects her ideas, but struggles to find her own true expression.

"It's Harder for Moms"

Daughters, like Lil, empathize with their mother's loss of live-in children and lack of direction. They understand that a mother may have a difficult time adjusting to the reality of an adult daughter or recognizing the fact that a daughter's decisions are valid. "I think the hardest thing for a mother is to go from a mother-child relationship to that of a friend," a 26-year-old said as she and her friends were discussing their mothers. "When you start taking responsibility for yourself, it's a type of transition. You have to be willing to open up to your parents and be honest with them about who you are and what you do, and that is hard. I think it's a lot harder for the parent to make the transition. I think they're sad because they're losing a child, and it's hard for them to be on a one-on-one friendship level. They've been a parent from day one, and they have to change. It's easier for a child, definitely."

Her friends agreed with her. They have come to a new understanding of themselves and their mothers—a realization that it's okay not to emulate a mother or even consider a mother a role model. Now they are more willing to look at their mothers objectively, to understand them within the context of the lives they've led. Objectivity and understanding did not surface in my interviews with adolescent girls. Adolescent girls freely criticized their mothers without attempting to understand a mother's motives, background, or the generational divide.

"I Wish My Mom Had Five Other Kids"

When daughters find themselves recipients of too much motherly attention, they sometimes don't know how to extricate themselves. Lindsay, an only daughter with one brother, often feels overwhelmed by her mother's intense desire to give her both emotional and financial support. She wishes her mother "had five other kids so she could give to them. It's hard being the only recipient." Catie's mother also wants to do everything for her, and Catie feels badly that she always is the receiver, not the giver. "My mom's a giver, which makes me feel sad. She'll do anything for us, and I feel bad sometimes because she's so nice."

These young women do not feel *enmeshed* (a therapist's word to describe overly connected mothers) or deprecate their mothers' capacity to love. Rather they listen to their mothers and still maintain their own sense of self. "It's not a control thing. My mom's not like that," noted Catie, whose mother is in the real estate business. Her mother had sensed her distress at not finding an apartment, located one for her, and put a deposit down on it. Her mother called her at work and said, "If you don't like it, I can get the security money back. You might even hate it, and I'm not going to feel bad if you hate it, but the apartment market is tight and I thought you may want it." Some daughters might have objected and considered such help to be interference. But Catie was grateful that her mother had helped out (and she liked the apartment).

When I asked these women how they could accept so much from their mothers and still consider themselves independent, they admitted it was a tough question. However, they all agreed that they were thinking of their mothers' feelings, wanting them to adjust to their being on their own.

"I do feel that I have enough independence," Catie

answered, "but my parents want to give us so much because they had to struggle financially for many years. They feel blessed that they can give to their kids and take a little of the pressures off. So I struggle with it. They give so much, but yet I want to be independent. Can I stand on my own two feet without them?"

Another woman expressed dismay at friends of hers who, at age 30, were still accepting money from their parents. She believes that "if you take money from your parents, you have to do what they say. They have something over you. If you don't take money from your parents, you are your own person."

If both mother and daughter freely discuss their feelings about finances (the mother's desire to help and the daughter's desire for independence), they usually find a common ground. For instance, if a daughter's health insurance is not covered by her work (as was the case with our daughters), one or both parents could cover that large expense. (This can be a security measure for parents as well since they might be held accountable for unexpected medical bills.) Each parent-daughter pair must work out a solution, but they definitely should consider a daughter's desire to be on her own and not indebted to her parents.

Young women often express appreciation for their mothers. "Her life has been her family," said Dawn, age 27, "and I think it's been hard for her to have her kids grow up and not need her. She's been a wonderful mother, but it's interesting because I'm of a different generation. I've got different interests. I've got a job that I love. Her focus was my father and her kids, and she has a tremendous amount of equal love for all of us."

These women clearly are looking at their mothers through nonadolescent eyes.

Respecting the Boundaries

My delight at listening to young women talk positively about their mothers was not tempered by their reluctance to reveal details about their intimate lives to their mothers or the need of some to set boundaries for their mothers. Although a few mothers complained that their daughters told them "too much," most young women I spoke with did not want their mothers to know everything.

"I think it's a generational thing," a 27-year-old said. "Our parents were raised in a courtship era. Things were different. I talk about my deep emotions with my mom—what I'm feeling or thinking—but I don't get into the physical things. When you're involved with someone, you really don't sit back and talk about the nitty-gritty."

A young woman's ability to distinguish herself from her mother, as indicated by her willingness to withhold information she considers private, confirms recent research.[3] In a Florida State University study, the researchers found that mothers and young adult-daughters are both "emotionally close and behaviorally independent of one another."[4] They can discuss deep feelings while maintaining the necessary boundaries between mother and daughter. They can set different standards of behavior for themselves yet remain affectionate and close.

One 23-year-old woman told me that "as I get older, I appreciate my mother's values. I'm happy that I have a mother-daughter relationship, not a friend relationship like some people who talk with their mothers about their sex lives."

Communication between a mother and daughter does not have to be "confessional," as seen, and sometimes admired, on afternoon talk shows. The desire to share lives, to discuss experiences, and to seek advice does not have to become complete disclosure. Respecting each other's privacy is paramount in a friendship between adults and should be primary in the friendship between mother and daughter.

When mothers don't respect boundaries and are too intrusive, daughters have to figure out ways to let them know the limits. "Sometimes it takes getting away from your parents for a while," said Marianne, who, after college, worked for a year on another coast. "When you're living in the same city, there are certain obligations and old habits that are still there. When you physically remove yourself, when you put miles between you, something happens." And that something often is a mother's recognition that her daughter is an adult, can manage her own income, her own household, her own problems.

Being Realistic

A daughter's honest view of her mother may include acknowledging her mother's weaknesses and strengths. Ingrid's mother is very opinionated. Ingrid acknowledged she herself is opinionated (her friends laughed in agreement) and likes a challenge, but she added that she also inherited from her father a softer and more understanding nature. Although Ingrid said her mother is "great" and has never pressured her, she admitted, "I've definitely learned to deal with her on a more patient level." Ingrid's assessment of her mother was both loving and realistic.

Nickie's mother is very "inquisitive." Nickie humors her by exaggerating her adventures, telling her "more than she wants to know": "Because she is so wonderful and she's really funny, I like to shock her in some ways because my life is so different than hers. She's living a little voyeuristically through me, so when I travel through the Mideast on business, I always make it sound scary, like bombs are blowing up. My poor mom is having a heart attack. I love to shake her up a little bit. She enjoys it, and I enjoy it. We probably talk once or twice a week."

Ingrid and Nickie love their mothers for who they are.

Wanting to Know a Mother

In a sample of employed health-care workers, researchers from the Center for Research on Women at Wellesley College found that by age 25, most employed adult daughters experience their relationships with their parents as primarily positive. The researchers noted that the popular image of "conflicted and damaging adult daughter-mother relationships are the exception, not the rule." Close relationships are the rule.[5]

And daughters and mothers want that close relationship. Jessica has thought a lot about her mother recently. During her adolescent years, her parents divorced, and she blamed her mother for her father's departure. But now as she approaches 30, she thinks she blamed her mother unjustly. "My mom is not as communicative as I think she should be, and I think that's the pattern she's fallen into with me. So I try to be more communicative and get things out. There's a lot about her I don't know, and I don't know if I will be able to pull it out of her. She's warm and generous and caring and loving, but I think there's a lot that she's felt and gone through and dealt with that I don't really understand because she hasn't talked about them."

Because Jessica's mother was raised in an era in which a person, particularly a woman, did not talk about disturbing feelings, Jessica feels as though she doesn't know her mother. Her mother's "communicative pattern" includes keeping a tight lid on her emotions. Now in her early sixties, her mother was born during the Great Depression, lived through three wars, and learned that a woman's role was to be the silent, supportive partner. Jessica wants to know what her mother thinks of her role and is trying to figure out ways to reach her. Because she and her mother do not live in the same area, her efforts may take longer than she hopes.

Many young women like Jessica have passed through a blaming stage, and now they look to mothers for friendship, beyond the confines of just mother-child. "I've never talked to my mother about what her dreams were, what her hopes were," said one 28-year-old. "I have this goal now of getting to know her for real. She's always been a good listener, but now I think she's giving us more of herself." She thinks her father has dominated the family and wants her mother to become more self-focused, to be there "for herself," to think of herself first for a change.

A daughter's yearning for her mother to step out of her shell, to speak up, to let herself be known stems from a daughter's need for a confirmation of her own life, her own sense of independence, her own finding of her voice.

"Please tell mothers that daughters need to learn from them that women have a relevance," a 23-year-old pleaded with me during a mother-daughter workshop I was leading. If a daughter has observed an unequal relationship between her mother and father, with her father excessively dominant or her father retreating when her mother was strong, she will wonder about her own role as a woman. The imprint of her mother's sense of self is particularly felt as she enters her years of single adult life. She needs to know that women's lives are important and that women grasp the significance of their contributions. These young women do not want diffident mothers: They want confident (but not overbearing) mothers.

Daughters who sense their mothers' self-confidence echo the words of one 26-year-old, who told me, "I love spending time with my mom." She is relieved that she doesn't have to worry about her mother. Her mother can take care of herself, so she feels free to enjoy her. "I talk with her more than twice a week," she reported about her "dynamic" mother, "and when she has a lot going on, maybe once a week."

A New Appreciation

After listening to mothers and daughters talk about the quality of their relationships, I realized that a new era of mother-daughter interactions has arrived. A young single woman is a new phenomenon in our society. She no longer exists solely as a "lady-in-waiting" for a groom, as her mother may have described her own decade of the twenties (if, indeed, she was not married already). These women value themselves, with or without a partner, and are intent on having their mothers understand their choices. They also are trying to unveil their mothers to get to know them better.

Their mothers' generation did not ponder what their own mothers were "really like." They accepted—or rejected—their mothers without too much concern about the influences that shaped them. Because these young women, at this point in their lives, have chosen different paths than their mothers (whether late marriage or cohabitation, delay of childbearing, career orientation), they are more aware of the contrasts between them. Their mothers knew they were going to follow their own mothers' footsteps with relatively early marriages. Childbearing would be a major focus of their lives, and work outside the home was viewed as a job, not particularly a career path.

Mothers of young-adult daughters want to have a different relationship with their daughters than they had with their own mothers. During the late sixties, they formed consciousness-raising groups to raise awareness of the status of women, and they often focused on their mothers' deficiencies. Their daughters have replaced consciousness-raising meetings with book groups, dinner gatherings, and a general reliance on friends to meet and discuss issues of concern. They do not center their conversations around their mothers' faults but tend to discuss them as women whose opinions they can accept or reject. Many daughters also discover that their mothers are really interesting individuals and want to know them better. Since understanding comes through communication, young women seem willing to spend unstructured time with their mothers.

As one woman said when she was describing a difficult time in her life, "It was enough to know my mother was psychologically in tune with me. Even if she couldn't understand, she would be understanding." That statement describes a true friend who knows how to communicate.

5

Boyfriends

Boyfriends

CC I'm only 22, so I'm not too worried about boyfriends," Amie said. "But the thought of being 26 or 27 and not dating anyone special is terrifying." Mari, age 27, agrees with Amie: "The thought of not getting married is my biggest nightmare." Amie and Mari's fear of not getting married is not shared by all young women. More independent-minded women are irritated by such lamentations and are less anxious about boyfriends. "If it happens, it happens" is their attitude.

Most young women, however, still envision marriage at some point in their lives. They describe marriage as a partnership where husband and wife "enhance" each other. Yet the ideal age for marrying has changed. "If someone could assure me that I would be married by age 35, I would relax," a 30-year-old woman confessed. She has plans of going to graduate school and beginning a new career, but she also wants assurance that a husband will be part of her future.

During the decade of her twenties, a young woman will drop old boyfriends, meet new ones, perhaps live with a boyfriend or get married. But the chances are she will not follow in her mother's footsteps and marry in her early twenties. No longer is she automatically engaged in her senior year. She chooses instead to enter the working world unattached and free. She wants to delay her wedding day.

The median age in the United States for a woman's first marriage has climbed to 24.5 years (26.7 years for men),[1] which means that half the women who marry for the first time are over the age of 24.5. This postponement of marriage adds another unknown to a woman's life. Along with the uncertainty about a career and a place to live, there is the question, which may grow to nag her as she nears 30, of whether or not she will meet a potential spouse.

But for now, in her early years out of college, she wants to live on her own, try out lifestyles, jobs, and locations.

Mothers' Reactions

Most mothers agree with their daughters' slower approach to marriage. They want their daughters to have careers, to be self-sufficient, to live on their own for a while, to grow in self-confidence. "My mom told me to wait till I'm 30," a young woman said. "She told me you have to do things on your own."

Most mothers believe that a good marriage, one in which spouses are friends as well as lovers, will give their daughters a secure base for developing themselves. They will have someone who truly believes in them. Mothers don't want their daughters to miss that opportunity.

One mother whose four daughters are in their late twenties and early thirties sometimes panics because she never hears them talk about marriage, even though two daughters have serious boyfriends. Although her daughters have achieved in the world of work and outwardly are satisfied with their living situations, she worries. She is concerned that the longer they postpone marriage, the less likely they are to marry. "They are so focused on careers," she said. "They're certainly not rushing into anything and seem not the least ready to make a commitment. They talk about having children. Having children is in their thoughts before they know exactly who they would like to have them with."

One of her daughters was engaged but broke off the engagement because she didn't know how she could fit marriage into her "too busy and too complicated" professional life. Her mother tries to assure her that she will figure it out, but she wonders if her daughter's frenetic lifestyle will ever allow the active participation of a husband.

Dodie, a woman in her early fifties, described another problem. Because her daughter has been involved in so many relationships, she worries that her daughter loves "too much." Dodie would like her daughter to be more comfortable with herself and not always feel it necessary to be with a boyfriend. But her daughter defends herself by saying she has many friends who are in long-term relationships or will marry before age 30. She does not want to be left behind. Having a boyfriend at all times makes her feel secure.

As much as mothers hope their daughters will find a mate for life, they have a difficult time knowing how to react to a new boyfriend. Daughters may have a succession of serious relationships, unlike the more formal "courtships" of the fifties and sixties. A mother who likes her daughter's choice and gets excited about the prospect of a fine son-in-law may find that when the relationship ends, she has to get used to a new choice. Conversely, she may have wasted time worrying about a boyfriend she disliked only to find that he disappears quickly from the scene.

Because of this uncertainty about their daughters' relationships, mothers cannot second-guess them or the boyfriends, so they try to be discreet when expressing their opinions. Daughters may interpret this caution as dislike or disinterest when, in reality, their mothers are keenly interested.

Mothers realize that a boyfriend or partner or husband can change the mother-daughter relationship and the dynamics of the family in general. One mother in her early fifties described having dinner with her daughter and her boyfriend, a young man whom her daughter had been dating consistently for four years. "His hand was on the table," she recalled, "and I remember staring at that hand thinking about what it was like to have your child bring a stranger into your family. I had this fantasy about this hand, where it had been on my daughter, what it had touched. What it would be like if he married my daughter. Would that alter my relationship with her? I thought about it for weeks after, just from his hand."

Mothers would like to talk honestly with their daughters about boyfriends, share their feelings, their own experiences, their wisdom about intimate relationships. But because so many mothers do not want to appear critical or give advice that could be construed as warnings (the way many of their mothers behaved toward them), they remain quiet. A mother of three daughters said longingly, "I wish my daughters would ask me my opinion about marriage, no strings attached. I would love to be able to have that dialogue with them about these issues. But I would not volunteer the information because I have to treat them like adults and they have to figure things out by themselves."

Some mothers can't keep still. Lynne, for instance, at first hesitated to talk with her daughter about her own experiences because she did not want to appear nosey or critical of her daughter's boyfriend (whom she did not like). But she herself, for many reasons—including her own remarriage—had been thinking about her own sexuality. After some thought, she decided to ask her daughter if she had ever had an orgasm. She wanted to share with her daughter her own evolution from discomfort with her body to full sexual enjoyment. When her daughter recovered from her surprise, they discussed the subject briefly and have never mentioned it again. Their relationship returned to their usual exchange of sharing information and ideas. Lynne is happy, however, that she broached the subject.

The mother of a 35-year-old single woman could not contain herself when her daughter commented that her current relationship did not have enough romance. "Honey," she exclaimed, "when you're 20, it's bells and whistles, not when you're 35." Another mother told me that she sat her daughter down and demanded to know when she and her boyfriend of six years would be engaged. They were engaged shortly after. A mother's comments may even make the newspaper. In a featured wedding story in the *New York Times*, a bride laughingly reported that her mother told her, "If you blow this one, don't bother coming home for Christmas again." When the couple at last became engaged, she said they called her mother first so she "could stop saying the rosary."[2]

How does a mother, a biased witness to her daughter's relationships, make judgments about her choice of men? I used to ask myself three questions whenever I met my daughters' new boyfriends: Does she seem happier with him than without him? Is she making good decisions about her life or career with him? Is he bringing out the best in her? Those questions are not always easy to answer because a daughter may be living in another city and the contact is mostly by phone. Or she may not be willing to talk about a boyfriend until she is confident that he will be around for a while. Or she may not want her mother to get too excited and push for wedding plans. But during a long relationship a mother usually can sense changes in her daughter and can answer those questions—even if her questions are never voiced.

Mothers who base their opinions of boyfriends on cultural, class, religious, or racial differences can be dead wrong about the durability, compatibility, and love of the relationship. All mothers can recall stories of their own generation when parents warned their daughters against a boyfriend because of ethnic or religious reasons and then regretted their words.

Young women do not make decisions about boyfriends light-heartedly, and mothers must trust their daughters' judgments. Only a daughter knows what is best for her, and after a few years of living on her own, she values even more the qualities of a real partner. Boyfriends come and go and a daughter may have many, but choosing a husband is a lifelong commitment. Only she can make the final choice. A mother can help by building her self-confidence and trusting in her decisions.

I am convinced that a good marriage offers a woman a plat-form for her work and family, a stability and a springboard that gives her strength to succeed as a mother, a business or profes-sional person, or in whatever other role she chooses. But she must select the man.

One mother expressed a thought that enters the minds of many mothers today: "I think there is a period of time when you are open to getting married, and then that passes." Her friend phrased it a little differently: "If they don't get married when they're youngish, then they get pickier and pickier. They care more about themselves, and they're looking for more in a guy."

The best way for daughters to gauge who has the potential attributes of a life partner is to meet and develop male friends. Mothers must be prepared to quietly observe the scene and hope for the best.

Daughters

The Social Scene

"How do you meet men?" I ask almost every young woman I meet. While their answers vary, they basically confirm that the indiscriminate meeting of men in bars has ended. They meet through other friends, blind dates, large parties, health centers, classes, work, and occasionally through a personal ad or Internet chat room. Although young women sometimes hang out at bars, they usually are accompanied by friends and are wary of someone who does not know any of the group.

When I asked a group of women, ages 28 to 30, how they meet men, they laughed and asked me to tell them. Their jobs don't offer social opportunities. Because of their erratic schedules, sometimes working until late at night, they cannot schedule regular events like tennis or health club workouts. So they rely on friends and weekend parties to meet new people, but they often have to force themselves to leave a cozy apartment and good book. "I could spend a whole weekend alone," a former model said. Because she wants to meet men, she goes out, but the process is not easy, and she concedes she may not seem approachable.

Her friends admitted that meeting others does not become easier the older and, yes, choosier they become. One of them said: "I unfortunately took self-sufficiency to such an extreme I cut people off. I think I finally have gotten to a place where I can make myself a little more vulnerable, open up a bit more because I'm not going to connect with anyone if I keep that wall." Now at age 30, she is more willing to be a little vulnerable, more flexible, and more reliant on friends and family.

Another woman said her male friends have told her that she gives the impression that she doesn't need to go out, that her life is busy and fulfilling without men. She claims, however, that she would never assume a man's life is too busy to include a woman: "I wouldn't offer myself up, but if a guy asked, 'What could I do Saturday night?' I would like to say, 'You could go out with me.'" But she doesn't say this because she is afraid of his response.

For these women, the dilemma is how much should they be

available and when, if ever, they should take the first step. They are cautious. "You don't want to be approachable because you don't want to have people reject you," one woman confided. "You don't want to put yourself up as available and be rejected and then feel awful. So it's almost easier to give the impression that you don't need that much."

Younger women, those just out of school, don't worry as much about meeting potential boyfriends. "This city [New York] is crawling with gorgeous men," exclaimed Eileen, age 23, who had recently moved to a new location. Her girlfriend, however, felt left out of the social scene because she has a boyfriend from college. But because of the abundance of new possibilities, she is thinking about dating again. This group of friends enjoy blind dates, arranged by friends or women in their offices, because it is a safe way to meet new people. They hesitate to walk into bars because it's "scary." (However, they noted that if they lived in a smaller city, they probably would date a man they met at a bar.) In a large city, a random male could be "unstable in the mind" or "sleep with you and never call," they said, and "Who wants that?"

Sex

The area that clearly differentiates daughters from their mothers is sex. As difficult it is for daughters to believe, many of their mothers were virgins when they were married. The lack of birth control, the social stigma attached to overt premarital sex, and an environment that championed marriage and family undoubtedly contributed to their mothers' early entry into marriage.

During the fifties and much of the sixties, a woman who was sexually active outside marriage was considered a "loose" woman. She was the exception rather than the rule. However, with the simultaneous advent of the birth control pill and political unrest during the middle to late sixties, many prevailing norms of behavior were rejected. Women from all socioeconomic levels found it permissible to engage openly in premarital sex. But most mothers, as one woman put it, had "a diploma in one hand and a marriage license in the other."

For daughters, however, a marriage license may be far in the future, and sex before marriage is taken as a norm in many close male-female relationships. When I asked young women if their mothers knew they were sexually active, they responded that they didn't discuss the issue with their mothers. Their attitude is "what they don't know won't hurt them."

Victoria said, as her friends shook their heads in amazement, "My parents only got married so they could have sex, because when my mom was growing up you had to be a virgin and only really horrible girls weren't."

Victoria lost her virginity at age 17. She ritualized her sexual initiation. "I asked my best friend if he wanted to lose his virginity with me," she said. "We had this great conversation, and he agreed. All day long I told everything to say good-bye to Victoria—the virgin. I was really histrionic about the whole thing." She told her mother that she and her friend were going to a midnight movie and wouldn't be home till about 2 A.M. Instead they climbed to the roof of a local middle school. "It was really romantic, even though there was no romance," she recalled. "We were up there, and everything happened. I came back and crept up the stairs to kiss my mom good night. She asked how the movie was, and I said it was great and kissed her on the cheek, but I went downstairs feeling so ashamed that I had lied to my mom." The next day she told her mother that she didn't go to the movies, that she had lost her virginity instead. Victoria remembered her mother looking at her in horror and saying, "Don't ever do it again." Victoria assured her, "I don't think you have to worry about that 'cause it's done. I've lost it." She had taken her favorite stuffed animal with her and had dressed all in white. "It was so melodramatic. I'll always remember it, and we're still good friends. We never had sex again. It was like we were going to do this for one another and birth one another into adulthood."

Victoria's loss-of-virginity story is unique. But by the time women reach their twenties, the great majority have had sexual intercourse. Some women I interviewed are already turned off on sex. They thought having sex would bring them happiness and a committed partner. They have been disappointed. Also, the fear of sexually transmitted diseases (STDs) has replaced their mothers' fear of pregnancy. These young women freely discuss their dread of AIDS and other STDs, and they are not alone in their fear. Young women writing about their disillusionment with the free-sex era of the last part of the twentieth century confess their feelings of betrayal that sex was billed as the ultimate symbol of freedom and happiness.[3] Their disenchantment with uncommitted sex, coupled with a concern about STDs, makes them cautious.

Most of the women I spoke with had taken the AIDS test— many at blood banks because they felt more comfortable giving blood than going to AIDS clinics.[4] When I asked groups of women if they would ask a man to take an AIDS test before they slept with him, most replied yes. One woman affirmed, "Absolutely without a question."

They vividly recalled when the "shadow" of AIDS fell on their social lives. "We always thought of it as something the gay community had to deal with," said Jane, age 28, "and it slowly dawned on many of us that lots of the people we were sleeping with could be bisexual or drug users and perhaps our community really wasn't so distinct from the other communities that were being affected. You could really detect a kind of chill in the air. It was at the time when many of my friends were getting into longer-term relationships. Suddenly you have to go to the clinic to get tested, and that's an absolutely terrifying experience."

One 29-year-old woman was tested twice, once after she

broke up with a drug-affected boyfriend and then again before she started dating her present boyfriend. She knew they were going to have a serious long-term relationship, and she was afraid of passing it on to someone she loved.

Another woman said her boyfriend had been tested because he had slept with a woman who literally had slept with "hundreds" of people.

The wariness about AIDS does not always filter down to other sexually transmitted diseases. Five out of the ten most common diseases reported to the Centers for Disease Control are STDs, with chlamydia being the most prevalent (four million cases a year).[5] The National Health and Social Life Survey, a probability sampling of 3,432 men and women ages 18 to 59, reported that the infection rate of STDs among 18- to 24-year-olds was higher than for any other age group.[6] Genital herpes is on the rise among adolescents and women in their twenties. These studies support the position of doctors who urge sexually active women to have annual gynecological checkups, no matter what their age. Chlamydia, for instance, often is asymptomatic and detected only through a medical screening.

The joy of sex has been tempered by statistics, and the sexual abandon of the seventies and early eighties is disappearing. "I just don't have sex anymore," said a 29-year-old. "I never really did have uncommitted sex, but now before I sleep with anyone we'll discuss AIDS."

"I was not promiscuous before," her friend added. "I always thought there was danger in sex." Before she lost her virginity at age 17, she looked up all the types of contraception and reported back to her boyfriend what they were going to use. She said she was raised with an immense amount of respect for herself. She was not going to get herself in a situation with someone who did not have respect for her.

These women now are older and wiser. When they discuss

boyfriends, they talk not just about sex, but about their desire for a truly loving and committed relationship between responsible partners who respect and support each other.

The Rules

The publication of the book *The Rules: Time-Tested Secrets for Capturing the Heart of Mr. Right* by Ellen Fein and Sherrie Schneider brought sarcastic comments from men and criticism from women who claimed the authors were turning the clock back to the fifties.[7] And when I read the book, most of the rules reminded me of the natural interactions that took place between men and women during the fifties and early sixties.

The authors of *The Rules* assert that men should take the lead in relationships. I understand and agree with the feminist complaint that this rule disregards the hard-fought attainment of equal status between the sexes. Some of the other rules struck me as conniving and less than honest. But I also agree with the authors that a female show of restraint is also a show of self-respect. Their thirty-five rules include not sitting around pining for a man but getting a life of "your own" by developing interests; not divulging everything about oneself in the first meetings; never dating married men; never counting on changing a man; not getting sexually involved right away. Let the man take the lead, they challenge, but slow him down.

Does the strategy recommended in *The Rules* encourage a woman to be too aloof or remote? Women who remain a little mysterious are much more enticing to men, according to the authors, and I am inclined to agree with them. Being mysterious does not mean being unapproachable, but it does mean owning a core of your self that will be revealed only to a man who is committed to you and in love with you. It means knowing that you are worth pursuing.

Some women have always received "go slow" messages from their mothers. Leslie described Rule 5 to perfection. "My mother always said you don't ever call boys," she told me and then laughed. "I still hear this residual. I never asked Mike out. I planned and manipulated and did everything that a southern woman does to get a man, without ever letting him know that I set it up. He was a marked man. I had decided the battle plan. I couldn't call him, as liberated as I feel. When it comes to relationships with men, I have my mother's voice in the back of my head saying, 'Don't call boys.'" Leslie said that when her friends do call men, they get "shafted." She claimed that a lot of men say they are flattered when a woman calls them, but when a woman does call, they get scared and back off, claiming she wants too much.

Another 30-year-old said that whenever she has asked a man out, she receives an excuse like "I have a girlfriend." She doesn't know if that is true or not. So she now hesitates before asking a man for a date. Being the instigator has not worked for her. In the working world, either a man or woman arranges a meeting or invites another for lunch—but business is not romance.

Even if the woman has taken the first step, men often like to take the next ones. A young married couple told me that they met on an airplane when she moved up to the empty seat next to him shortly before their flight landed. She had been watching him, observed that he did not wear a wedding ring, waited until he finished working, and then slipped in next to him and initiated a conversation. He found out where she was staying but thought he would never see her again. But as he was bragging to his friend who met him at the airport about how enticing he was to women, he noticed that she was embracing a tall, handsome man. At that moment he decided to pursue her. The competitor in him spurred him on. He became the initiator.

A New Appreciation of Self

"I saw my old boyfriend the other day," Karen, age 28, said, "and I can't believe I wasted seven years of my life on him." The others in the room shared Karen's feelings as they told similar stories of old boyfriends. Their tastes changed because they had changed. They were more sure of themselves and no longer needed a boyfriend to make them look good. Karen's sense of self was strengthened by the challenges she found at work, her explorations of other cities, and her encounters with new friends.

Her friend, Emily, told of how drained she felt from her boyfriend who followed her to new cities for a few years after college. "I would lose myself in that relationship. I wanted to fix him to the point where I had to ask myself what I was doing. I was becoming mean and hateful. You can't fix someone else. I didn't like the way I sounded, and I didn't want to fix someone else. It was so liberating when we broke up."

Emily, who is now engaged (to someone else), talked about her relationship with her fiancé." I never worry about trying to fix him at all. It's not draining. We can both do our own thing, but we love each other very much and are supportive of each other."

These women found that being on their own for a while—without serious boyfriends—helped them develop themselves. Now they find that when they get into a relationship, they have an easier time saying who they are. "I never used to say I liked classical music," Emily said, "and now I can say it and go into the other room to listen."

Twenty-five-year-old Caitlin claimed that 24 was her most difficult year. She ended the most serious relationship she ever had, and it took her a year to get over it. Although her ex-boyfriend was a "wonderful person" and taught her how to laugh and was there for her during the difficult transitional period from college to work, they hung on too long. But she now says, "I finally came to terms with the fact that I loved him but I wasn't in love with him."

Naomi related a similar story of joy and relief when her first real relationship ended. They had stayed together longer than she wanted to because he loved her so much. When they at last broke up, they only stayed apart for a short time, came back together, and spent sort of a two-month "honeymoon period." But then she discovered all the problems that were there before were still present; nothing had changed. She was pouring every ounce of energy into a relationship that wasn't beneficial to her, but she didn't want to admit it. She kept telling everybody that it was great, but deep down she knew she wasn't happy. When she finally "let go," she felt so much better. She was running one day with a friend, who commented on how much happier she looked. "I had no idea what I was doing to myself," she recalled. "I'm like a whole new person."

Karen summed up why some, perhaps many, women fall for the wrong man when they are young: "I really thought if you loved someone enough and you were there for them and supportive and provided a good example, they would rise to the occasion and change. That's a big lesson I learned in my early twenties. I had a lot of loser boyfriends. I don't know how I could have been so self-abasing. I only got depressed and had lots of heartaches. It made me appreciate Jack [her present boyfriend], who I may not have appreciated as much if I hadn't been through the stuff I have."

These women learned from experience that boyfriends who sap energy require a lot of maintenance and do not lead to a true connection. They also found that when they broke up, they could stand on their own and had more time to focus on their own growth. At first they feared that they would never meet another man. Now they feel good about the decision and better about themselves, a sign of maturity and mental health.

Good mental health goes hand in hand with the ability to

concentrate on the present. Fretting about what may or may not happen creates anxiety and also casts a shadow on the present. Focusing on the present does not exclude planning for the future, looking for opportunities for growth, or thinking about a date on the weekend. However, needless concern about a vague possible happening or nonhappening (like never meeting a mate) is deadly.

Cohabitation

Another distinguishing marker between the mothers' and daughters' generations is the growing phenomenon known as cohabitation—unmarried couples living together. Today, in the population under age 25, 1.2 million households describe themselves as cohabitating, and in the population between the ages of 25 and 34, 2.1 million are cohabitating. (The Census Bureau calls such individuals *POSSLQs*—persons of opposite sex sharing living quarters.)[8] When these figures are compared with the 1970 and 1980 numbers of cohabitating households of all persons over the age 19 (500,000 households in 1970 and 1.6 million households in 1980),[9] it is clear that the movement is toward more, rather than less, cohabitation. Not all of these households consist of paired couples, but the trend for couples to live together is on the rise.

For most young couples, living together has not replaced marriage but is a prelude to marriage. About half of all cohabitating couples either marry or break up within eighteen months, and 90 percent break up within five years. When cohabitation ends, an estimated 60 percent of the couples marry each other, and 40 percent end their relationship.[10] Some move in together when they become engaged, while others have not discussed marriage but seem to be testing their compatibility.

Most of the research on this topic reports that unions preceded by cohabitation are associated with "lower quality of marriage, lower commitment to the institution of marriage, greater likelihood of divorce than couples who did not cohabitate."[11] However, much of that research examines persons born between 1928 and 1957, when cohabitation before marriage was more common among persons who had little education and low incomes. Not until the seventies did cohabitation begin increasing for all educational and income levels.[12]

More recent research that compared the relationship quality of cohabitating and married partners found that while cohabitators in general reported poorer relationship quality than their married counterparts, the cohabitators who plan to marry are not significantly different from married couples.[13] However, other research has observed that attitudes toward sexual exclusivity differ between cohabitating and married couples. Cohabitating couples behave more like dating couples in that they are more willing to have another sexual partner outside the primary relationship. This study confirmed others that suggest those who cohabitate may be less inclined to commit and tend to value independence rather than interdependence.[14]

The attitude of young women toward living with their boyfriends vary. Many would hesitate to move in with a boyfriend because of their parents' disapproval; if they do move in together, they conceal the arrangement from their parents. One woman installed a separate phone line so her boyfriend wouldn't have to answer the phone.

A woman in a long-term relationship said she and her boyfriend were not living together out of respect for his mother, who would be very upset by such an arrangement. Another told me she would never live with her boyfriend before marriage because "a lot of the fun of marriage is getting to live with the one you love." Many do not live together because of their religious beliefs.

Two 30-year-old women who were living with their

boyfriends said they would get married only if and when they wanted children. When Tammie told her mother that marriage was not for her, her mother took it as a personal rejection. "My mom feels the same way," said her friend. "My mom's favorite phrase about living together is 'Why buy the cow when you can get the milk for free?' "

"My mom has this notion that your worth to a man is in your virginity, and if you give that up you can only hope for the dregs of society," interjected a third woman.

Yet another woman, whose parents repeatedly separated when she was young and finally got divorced, reported that her mother told her, "If you ever think about getting married, live with a man first."

Strong sentiments exist on both sides of this issue. Many women may spend almost every night with their boyfriends but won't move in, while others consider living together one step toward marriage. Convenience and economics are often cited as the reasons to live together.

If a cohabiting couple marry because they think that marriage will fix a relationship that is floundering, their marriage is not likely to survive. The marriages of mothers who wedded in haste to have sex probably have not survived either. People marry because they love each other and want to commit themselves to a life together, not to improve their relationship.

The Woman-Man Connection

Countless therapists have tried to figure out the qualities of successful couples. Why do some couple thrive and find harmony with each other, while other couples "drain" each other, lose their vitality, and grow apart? To investigate that question, Stephen J. Bergman and Janet Surrey of the Stone Center at Wellesley College created a workshop format that brought men and women together to discuss the impact of gender differences in relationships. They explored ways to create "mutuality in male-female relationships."[15]

Finding new ways to nourish mutual love is especially timely now that a daughter's expectation of a spouse's role in marriage is different than her mother's. Most mothers assumed that they would have primary responsibility for the care of home and children, even if they and their spouses both worked. Their husbands would concentrate on life outside the home (work, the backyard, and the garage). They did not expect their husbands to be equal partners in the care of the family, to share in the diapering, the cooking, the washing. Their daughters, however, assume that their partners will share in the daily work of the home. Even though studies document that women still bear the major responsibility for the home, women always hope their husbands will be true partners.

The Stone Center workshops, called Creating Mutuality, acknowledge that men and women often view their relationship through different lenses. Bergman and Surrey led men and women through a series of questions and discussions (first segregated into male and female groups and then together) about what they would like to know about the other gender. Sometimes the dialogue between the men and women became very heated, but the leaders encouraged them to "stay with the conflict and stay with the connection." As the couples moved beyond "you" and "me" to "we," a feeling of mutual responsibility for the relationship arose.

Many young women (perhaps all women) are baffled by their male counterparts. A dialogue that centers on mutual understanding—rather than attempting a one-way effort to have men understand women (or women understand men)—is helpful in building a better relationship. While women sometimes reveal their inner needs to their partners (the need to relate, to be listened to), men seldom open up and tell their partners what they want them to know.

When a group of men in the workshop were asked, "What do you most want women to understand about you?" they responded, "I am not your enemy; that many of my actions are acts of love; my difficulties communicating feelings; my need for solitude; my difficulties in admitting powerlessness and asking for help; that I need space; that I need time; I'm scared too; not to have to censor my maleness; that I love competition and play; how I feel about responsibility; the heavy burden placed on men to be successful and not look foolish; that being a son is often difficult; my sense of intrusion that often comes with relationships and my sense of shame for feeling that; I want to change; we care about relationships as much as women do; men are scared of other men too; that men have different priorities; the complexity of masculinity; our relational yearnings; our grief over losses; that I will come back after I go away."[16]

These acknowledgments comprise a powerful list. They reveal the underlying feelings responsible for actions that can be misinterpreted by women as rejection or disinterest. An honest effort by men and women to see another meaning, the intended meaning, behind behavior that causes misunderstanding will benefit their relationship. Women also have to bear in mind that men usually have difficulty discerning a woman's motivations. They cannot pick up hidden messages the way women do. Directness works better with men, not subtleties.

Psychological studies, such as the one from Wellesley, confirm good common sense. If a couple enjoy each other's company, share many interests, want to understand and bring out the best in each other, they are good candidates for marriage.

Elysa, age 30, and her fiancé exemplify the ease and sharing that can develop between a couple who are moving toward mutuality. "We were best friends when I was still dating a guy long distance," she told me. "After that broke up, we started dating almost immediately." After they were dating for about six months, they were talking about how they loved being with each other and how great that felt. Then her boyfriend said, "There's one thing we have never talked about." Elysa knew what he was referring to, but responded that she didn't think they were ready to talk about that yet, and he agreed.

A few months later, Elysa planned a special night, bought him a nice present, and asked him to marry her. "We hadn't talked about it directly, so it was kind of scary," she said. But because he had mentioned the subject first, she suspected he would accept her proposal. He did, and they became engaged.

A 27-year-old woman said she and a college friend kept track of each other through the years, occasionally catching up when he would come to her town. Recently, he told her that he had always admired her, thought of her a lot, and wanted to start dating. At first she thought he was joking, but now they are happily dating and he is arranging to move to her area.

Each couple can relate their own unique story of meeting and falling in love, and those stories are frequently told. "How did you meet?" is often the first question young couples are asked. They love recalling the event. The possibilities for meeting a potential boyfriend are endless. Finding the social opportunities in which a woman is most comfortable and self-confident is the challenge.

Finding Her Own Path

An increasing number of women will not marry, some by choice and some from lack of a partner. Their decision should be respected by mothers, and both mothers and fathers can reduce the pressure by not asking the questions that make their daughters uncomfortable. Women under the age of 25 don't seem to receive many comments from their parents, but over 25, parents get nervous.

"My mother knows better than to give me pressure," said a 30-year-old who lives with her boyfriend. Another young woman said that her mother never asked about marriage until she was 27. Her mother, up to that time, admired her daughter's career orientation, but as she came closer to 30, her mother got worried.

Some feel pressure from their fathers. "The only pressure I got was from my stepfather, who thought I wasn't smart enough to have a career," said another 30-year-old (who has a very prestigious job). "He would tell me to get married, just get married. He lives in a totally different generation, and I never really took it to heart."

Fathers also can be more accepting. Cissy recalled that her father told her that it didn't make any difference to him whether she was a single or married, whether she had children or not because she was the important person in his life. Whatever made her happy would make him happy. When I asked Cissy if she liked her father's comment, she replied, "It was almost like he was assuming I wouldn't get married, and he was giving me permission not to. So I acted sort of defensively. 'What are you saying? Do you think I'm doomed to be single?' "

Cissy's retort shows why parents (especially mothers who may comment offhandedly) have a difficult time broaching the subject of boyfriends to almost 30-year-old (or older) daughters. Whatever they say may be interpreted as pressure to marry, a sanctioning of a current boyfriend, or a general dissatisfaction with their daughters' love life. Perhaps the best thing mothers can do is to love their daughters unconditionally and let them find their own way.

Daughters who are mature want men who will enhance rather than drain, share rather than assign, seek mutuality rather than individual satisfaction. These men are worth waiting for.

6

The Midtwenties:
The End of
Option Paralysis

Moving into a Career

Sometime in her midtwenties, a young woman grows restless, realizes that her job is leading nowhere, and begins planning for the future. Up to now she may have avoided dramatic changes in her working life because of her inexperience with other careers and her relief that she has any job. But now as she passes the quarter-of-a-century mark, she recovers from *option paralysis*—a term used by one 27-year-old to describe her dismay at facing too many options—and begins to think "career," not "job."

A career frame of mind focuses a young woman who may have drifted through her first years out of college. Even though she supported herself (with a little help from parents) and lived independently, the malaise she experienced as she lost the support and structure of college lingered during the first years on her own. But during her midtwenties, resolve replaces uncertainty as she makes decisions, takes her career seriously, and settles on a place of residence.

Although the term *young adult* theoretically describes the

years between 20 and 30, a few women extend their adolescence into a stage called *youth*, prolonging their reluctance to commit to a job, a person, a cause. These women need extra years to develop a sense of themselves, to reconcile what they want to do with a realistic assessment of what they are capable of doing. When these "youth" lose their dreamlike expectations and recognize the reality and hard work of career development, they move into adulthood.

"Founding a family and building a career are the requirements for being accepted as an adult," writes Gene Bocknek in his book *The Young Adult: Development After Adolescence.*[1] Most researchers in human development single out the ability to make personal commitments as a hallmark of maturity. In their personal lives and in their working lives, young women in the midtwenties become more interested in career and long-term relationships.

Erik Erikson described young adulthood in the same context of work and family. "In young adulthood," wrote Erikson, "you learn whom you care to be with—at work and in private life."[2] Young-adult women become more discriminating, at work and with friends. Now they are willing to find work that has a future and requires commitment.

"I definitely would like to find a job that I cared about so I [would] want to work on a Saturday or Sunday or stay late on a Friday," said Connie, age 26. "It would be great to have a job you could feel so dedicated to." While they were willing to work at "nothing jobs" when they were adjusting to life outside school, they now are bored and restless. Connie's friend summed up her new resolution: "It's time for me to get involved in something else. I'm in this hole every day, and it's ridiculous and it's boring."

Both Connie and her friend have fairly good jobs. But the companies do not match their interests or talents. One works in the fashion industry and is tired of promoting lingerie styles. The other works with children but is trained as an art historian. They took jobs quickly because they wanted to pay off debts and live on their own, but now they want to step back and find careers that match their aptitudes.

"I Feel Like a True Young Adult"

Ellen, age 26, looked serious as she and her friends discussed their careers. Then she glanced around the room and said, "I think this year for the first time I feel like a true young adult. Before that I felt lost." Her friends nodded, acknowledging similar feelings. As a young adult, Ellen understands that her decisions are in her own hands, that she has control of her life. No longer "lost," but still mindful of the influence that friends and family (especially her mother) have on her, she now feels ready to say, "Yes, this is what I want to do."

A woman in her midtwenties is willing to ask, "What am I?" as well as, "Who am I?" Am I a teacher, a fashion designer, a broadcaster, a producer, a doctor, a lawyer, a social worker, a businesswoman? These questions energize her, and sometimes depress her, as she passes age 25. Wondering how she fits into society is another sign of her adult status.

One daughter described her early twenties as being her "limbo" years. Now, at 26, she feels on firmer ground with a career goal. She summarized her personal growth as follows: "I've learned to take things day by day and laugh at life a little. I've learned to focus more, and I'm not as flaky. I think on deeper levels, and I'm definitely calmer and more sound." Her mother cautions her that the twenties are the worst years for women and advises her to look forward to her thirties, when everything comes into balance. But she is not waiting for the next decade to get out of limbo. She is making good moves now.

Making Money

For years it was women who worked in lower-paid helping professionals like teaching, nursing, social work. But now making money is an incentive for some women to take their careers seriously. As women see friends being offered high salaries in business, finance, or as professionals, they see possibilities for themselves.

"I definitely want to make money," said a woman who will not enter her family business because she does not want to work on a commission-only basis. By the time women approach 30, they want jobs that will provide enough money to furnish an apartment with new rather than hand-me-down furniture, to travel, take vacations, and build an investment portfolio as well as a wardrobe.

One young woman has dreamed of owning a red Jaguar since she was a teenager working in a deli and admired a customer's "Jag." When an older gentleman, a customer at the store, told her all she had to do was marry a rich man and let him buy her a red Jag, she was incensed. Even though she was only 16, she looked at him and said, "No way. I'm going to get a job, and I'm going to have a career, and I'm going to buy my own Jag. I don't need my husband to buy one for me." Although she now is 25 and does not own her dream car, she will.

I was intrigued by some young women's honest approach to making money. "I don't want to be ungodly wealthy, but there are certain things I really like that are expensive," said one graduate business student. Women, like this one, who have grown up in comfort do not want to change their style of living.

"I *do* want to be ungodly wealthy and be able to do anything I want when I want—and help other people," said Cassie, her business school friend who comes from a family of professionals. "I think wealth gives you power and also time. If you have time and you want to donate to charity or work at a charity, you can do it."

Not everyone thinks in such expansive terms, and not everyone relates careers to money. For most young women, their primary motivation is to like their work, to immerse themselves in a career, and to advance in their chosen field. "It's the gratification of knowing you can do it more than the material benefits," said one. The many young women who work in nonprofit organizations, social services, or education demonstrate that women still want to enter the helping professions. They want to work with children or adults and help improve society.

Like Their Mothers?

Whereas mothers have typically been more connected to family life than to careers, their young-adult daughters show equal interest in both career and home, according to a study from the University of Missouri.[3] This trend among daughters is not surprising since young women have more career opportunities than their mothers did. Daughters also tend to receive emotional support from friends to pursue both paths, while their mothers felt emotional reinforcement for their role within the family and often received censure for work outside the home.

A 54-year-old mother who became a lawyer when her children were young received no reinforcement from professional colleagues. "I felt terrible pressure during interviews," she said. "They asked me all kinds of questions they had no business asking, like what kind of birth control I was using and whether or not I was going to be able to handle my kids." She recalled being interviewed by a state senate committee for a confirmation of a gubernatorial appointment and being lambasted for twenty-five or thirty minutes because she was too young, was a woman, and should be home with the children. One of the committee members even proclaimed that the governor had no business appointing someone who had children. She was eventually appointed, but the experience "stunned" her. Later she argued a case at the U.S. Supreme Court and found that the sign on the bathroom door in the attorneys' waiting room said "men only." When Sandra Day O'Connor was appointed to the Supreme Court, she wrote to the new justice suggesting that a lock be installed on the door and the wording be changed to "attorneys' bathroom."

Daughters may be "stunned" to realize that not too many years ago these types of obstacles were routinely placed in the paths of women who wished to pursue both family and career. But, thankfully, the atmosphere for women has changed dramatically since their mothers' time. Now more is expected of daughters, and they want to live up to others' expectations for them.

A study from Cornell University noted the power of the "gender role revolution" in framing women's attitudes. The researchers found that regardless of their mothers' attitudes toward work, daughters are more likely to work continuously, to hold professional jobs, to delay marriage, and to have fewer children.[4] Daughters in this study had an image of themselves as salaried workers more than homemakers. The researchers also found that the mothers' attitudes about women's work roles changed between the first time the mothers were contacted in the fifties and their final interview thirty years later. They too were more accepting of women in working roles. Mothers and daughters hold more similar views today.

As women, and men, accept more readily the idea of women in positions of power outside the home, mothers start imagining their own daughters in such positions. Many mothers of young girls now say, "She will be president." They visualize their daughters breaking through the male barriers.

Some older mothers never made that leap. Joan, a woman in her late forties who has successfully broken through the glass ceiling and is a well-known CEO, told me that her mother never commented on her success, even though she was the subject of many news stories. Only after her mother's death, when Joan was cleaning out her mother's house, did she find the news clippings stored in a dresser drawer. Secretly her mother was proud of her accomplishments, but the impression she gave Joan was that she just wanted grandchildren.

Daughters, even successful ones such as Joan, continue to hunger for their mothers' approval. The *Wall Street Journal* interviewed women who had started their own businesses, and one commented to the reporter, "My mother is proud of me. I'm going to be 40 years old and that still means so much."[5]

Mothers of daughters in their twenties will be more likely to express pride in the achievements of their daughters than did mothers a decade or so ago. They have encouraged their daughters along the way and will not hesitate to show their pride when the daughters succeed.

Mentoring

A debate about the quality of 20- to 30-year-old employees swirled in the pages of *Fortune* magazine. "Gen X" workers are arrogant, according to one reader, and disrespectful. The magazine was inundated with responses, some agreeing with the disgruntled employer and others defending young employees.

One journalist at *Forbes* summed up the reactions she received from young employees: "Hey, we are the children of divorce and upheaval and whirlwind technological change and we come straight out of an educational environment that is competitive to the point of lunacy. And we don't necessarily want to pay our dues by doing scutwork for years and years, because we watched our parents do that and then get laid off. So, yeah, we know we're no day at the beach. But we're pretty smart and if you try just a little harder to understand us, we promise you won't be sorry."[6]

I agree with part of the journalist's summary. These young women are smart, eager, and will not be ignored. However, to bring forth the best in young employees, companies need to supply mentors who will guide them and capture their natural enthusiasm and energy. When women managers were scarce, a young female employee often felt left out of the advancement loop and could not find a male manager who would guide her. She was likely to be overlooked for a promotion, even though she had the aptitude and skills for the job. But now, with many more women in management positions and male managers realizing that women will move up the ladder alongside—or ahead of—them, a young woman can more easily find a mentor.

When I met recently with four women entrepreneurs, each told a different story of success, but their one commonality was the use of mentors, both male and female, who had given them advice at crucial stages of their careers. They learned how to ask the right questions and how to position themselves for promotions. They also took risks, financial and personal, that paid off. When they started their own businesses, they applied the lessons they had learned from their mentors. And now they in turn are guiding young women who want to start their own businesses.

The 20- to 30-year-old woman who is looking for a mentor is likely to call a successful woman in her office a "role model." The younger woman will watch the older woman for clues about how to succeed at work and at home. The most attractive role model is one who manages both home and career successfully, and a young woman will want to talk with such a woman about how she manages to pull this off.

"I think I was about 25 when I started to grow up," confessed Daphne, age 30. "It's also when I got my first full-time job and dropped my loser boyfriend. Something clicked. I ended up with a great boss, and she is very determined and courageous and bold and smart. So she was this adult role model for me."

Daphne's boss and role model, who is very successful and respected in her field, works full-time but always leaves the office in time to be home for dinner with her children, and one day a week she works out of her home. She talked with Daphne about developing her writing skills, which Daphne was underutilizing in her job. Motivated by her boss's stated desire to read her literary attempts, Daphne started writing before and after working hours and now is a published writer. Her boss showed her that working hard at her daytime job does not exclude having a life outside the office.

Dee, who is 27, described her two mentors: "I've worked for two women, one near 60 and one who is 36. They're both very bright, family and career oriented, very diligent, and intelligent. I've liked working for these strong women, and they took me under their wings and have done their best to train me." She chuckled as she described a recent phone call with one of these mentors, who is no longer her boss: "She told me I was sounding more and more like her, and I said, 'Well, you've trained me, so if I end up being a pushy woman, it's all your fault. You'll have to deal with it.'"

Dee's assertion that she will turn into a pushy woman strikes at the heart of an oft expressed fear: Success means looking aggressive. As much as I thought that young women no longer fear that label, I found that many still hesitate to speak out in public, afraid of using their voices. In a recent news story, I was pleased to read that Secretary of State Madeleine Albright used to coach her female graduate students to speak up. "Women often wait too long in meetings to make their voices known," she told an interviewer. "And then, all of a sudden some man says whatever it is that you were going to say and everybody thinks it's brilliant."[7] Mentors can teach young women that participating fully in discussions means not holding back good ideas.

Men have always known the advantage of a mentor. "Hook yourself to a rising star" was the advice given to male graduates. "As he rises in the company, so shall you." Because women previously had not climbed the corporate ladder as quickly as men, they were not in the position to mentor young women. But now they are.

More than ever before, companies are devoting time, money, and energy to encourage full participation of women within their corporations. The print media also are recognizing the forward thrust of women into executive positions. Women's success stories are regularly featured in their pages. A *Businessweek* cover story highlighted six companies where "diversity gets top billing," detailing the efforts of these companies to mentor and develop women managers.[8] Although women executives still are rare enough to be deemed newsworthy, young women see opportunities for advancement in most business and are confident that their generation will not be blocked by a glass ceiling.

Companies should take note of recent research that found that both men and women intend to stay longer at a company if they perceive the work environment to be friendly to women.[9] A company that respects and acknowledges its women employees on the same basis as men will be rewarded by both male and female employee loyalty.

Daughters Do It Their Way

"I first was into architecture and that was creative, and my mother said, 'Why don't you get into computers?' and then I went into film and she said, 'Why don't you go back to architecture?' She always wanted my life to be protected and not to struggle." Deana's mother was sure the entertainment industry would corrupt her daughter or at least expose her to influences that were not safe. Deana, now 28, is combining her architectural, computer, and filming skills as a sought-after camera person and hopes to become a director. "My mom had a hard time with the letting-go stage," she said. "She wants me to be independent and go off on my own and have a good life, except the reality is that she is not going to have control over my decisions and she's uncomfortable with that."

Deana's mother needs to realize that her daughter's choice of career is hers alone, guided only with an advice-when-asked policy from her parents.

Daughters sometimes receive less pressure than sons to enter a certain field or go into a family business. So they feel freer to pursue their own interests and find their own career path. Even when they ask for advice, their mothers must let them take the lead in planning their future.

Outside of the corporate setting, many women are creating their own businesses and filling niches in markets from their own homes. "We are the generation of the computer and the modem. Distance has no meaning anymore," a 33-year-old commented to a reporter.[10] The computer allows women to keep connected to offices or start their own enterprises, but young women entering the workforce usually have to learn the intricacies of business before they can branch out on their own. Many anticipate being independent entrepreneurs, often for the purpose of combining family and career. In the meantime they must learn the tools of business.

"There are things I would love to accomplish, but now I'm enjoying the process. My income is low, but I feel I'm at a learning phase. There are creative things I want to develop, but for now I have to balance my creative urges with the need to make money." This comment by a 27-year-old woman sums up the feelings of many young women who want to work in the arts, write, paint, design, refinish furniture. As soon as they learn business techniques and save some money, they would like to work independently.

When I asked a young woman to describe her role model, she named Toni Morrison because Morrison was a struggling mother with three children and wrote a Pulitzer Prize-winning novel. "So I have this picture in my head," she said, "of my sitting at home at my computer writing and telling the kids to be quiet so I can concentrate."

Young women whose mothers may not have worked during their childhood see their careers as bringing a fuller aspect to their own lives. They don't necessarily think their mothers missed out because they didn't work, and most appreciate their mothers' dedication to family. "My mother didn't sacrifice her life for us," said one woman. "She wanted children and was very happy. I don't think she felt she was missing out on a career. She enjoyed us, and when we would go away to camp, she would take classes and sometimes she would substitute-teach." This young woman looks at her mother as a role model for family life and seeks out others as mentors for her work life.

Doing What She Likes

When they find careers that suit their talents, daughters can't believe their good luck. A woman described a day in her working life in which she was sitting on a balcony overlooking the ocean and reading a novel that she was evaluating for her boss. "I stopped halfway through the book," she said, "and I was lounging on a couch eating bonbons, flipping through this book, and I thought, I can't believe I'm reading for a living. Reading is my favorite thing in the planet, and here is someone giving me a paycheck to do this."

Everyone can relate to that—getting paid for doing what one

loves. Finding that perfect job is not always easy, but a mentor can help a young woman search out a job that will utilize her aptitudes and, thereby, reduce her stress.

If a woman's ideal job is reading and writing summaries of novels to be evaluated for potential films, she should stay away from a repetitive job. A fit between job and person can be found, but the search takes time and sometimes includes going back to school.

Back to School

Many graduate schools now prefer students who have worked for a few years after earning their undergraduate degree. Students arrive with more focus on a career and a practical knowledge of a work environment. However, the loss of income and the added debt for graduate-student loans put a financial burden on a student, so she wants to be sure her extra degree will lead to better employment opportunities.

Many mothers also are returning to school to prepare for midlife careers, and often mother and daughter will be in school at the same time, different locations perhaps, but both committed to change. One may be enrolled part-time and the other full-time, but the desire to prepare for the next phase of their lives is the same.

"If you don't have specific training or a skill, you'll be someone's assistant. You need a graduate degree," complained one young woman with an undergraduate biology degree. She was applying to business schools and wants to work in the health field.

Angie already has a master's degree but found that her specialty in languages didn't prepare her for a job. She worked overseas for a while, tried a few other jobs, and ended up in retail sales. But as she approached 30, she at last admitted to herself that she always wanted to teach. Her family of "overachievers" earlier had dissuaded her from entering teaching because they did not consider teaching the profession for her. They wanted her to become a doctor or a business executive. Angie, therefore, delayed informing them of her plans until she was accepted in a Master's in Teaching program. She knew they would disapprove and think she was just jumping aimlessly to something else. But Angie is feeling more confident now that she is 30 and is ecstatic about her decision. "I'm very excited about it," she said. "I'm terrified of going back to school, but I'm really looking forward to teaching secondary school."

Many graduate students arrive at their decisions to return to school the way Angie did. Their first jobs were unsatisfactory. Others like their jobs and realize that they will not advance until they obtain that extra degree. Now they are willing to forego income and apply for more loans or prevail upon their parents for tuition. Despite increasing costs, young women are attending law school, medical schools, business schools in record numbers.

A group of law students, typical of graduate students everywhere, offered a variety of reasons for wanting a law degree. A law course in college piqued Lynda's interest, and she sought out a job as a paralegal to test the profession. When I asked her if she liked what she saw in the law firm, she replied that she really did not like working as a paralegal because she acted as a secretary and baby-sitter for the lawyer. But in spite of all the nitty-gritty work she performed, she still decided to apply to law school. Her previous jobs in retail and banking did not offer her the same path to the success that she sees for herself.

"I had a couple of internships during college and met a lot of lawyers who advised me not to go to law school," Lynda's friend said. "After graduation I worked for a state representative and decided I loved the policy side of government and saw that having a law degree would help me a lot. It also is a viable path to a certain income level and a certain security. There's a tension between wanting a job that will be lucrative and a job that may be more policy making. I continue to struggle with how I am going to resolve that."

These young women know that once they commit to graduate school they must be successful, and in law school that means three years of intensive training. Another student commented, "During the first year, it was beyond me how anyone who was not 100 percent sure could ever do this because I was pushed. I never doubted that this was what I wanted to do, even though I often cried with the stress. It was just a matter of getting to that goal. I can see how people drop out because why would you put yourself through that if you weren't sure."

During the stress and hard work of graduate school, some daughters call upon their mothers for moral support. One woman called her mother daily during her first year of medical school, and her mother assured her that she would do well because she had always done well. "Don't you realize," she said to her mother, "that every student's mother can say the exact same thing? And when a professor marks on the curve, someone has to be at the bottom of the pile, and there's no reason to think I'm more special than anyone else."

"I felt my whole identity was grades," moaned another woman who had successfully finished her second year of law school. But she brightened up and admitted that her one bad grade in her first year did not jeopardize her acceptance at a well-known law firm, although the interviewer asked her specifically about that grade.

Sometimes a member of a woman's family sets the example of the profession. Many male physicians' sons used to enter the field of medicine, and now so do their daughters. Professions open to mothers often did not include law or medicine. Most women entered law or business as secretaries and medicine as nurses. In contrast, their daughters may choose any position in any field.

"As long as I can remember, I wanted to come to law school," said Mindy. "My brother is ten years older, and when he was in law school I knew I wanted to be like him. The expectation from my family was not for law per se but for some professional career." Mindy's mother, who is in her seventies, went to medical school as a young woman when there were few women physicians. She practiced while raising a large family and serves as her daughter's role model for a successful professional woman and mother.

My own daughters entered graduate schools after pursuing careers "in the field." After dancing professionally for ten years, my older daughter returned to undergraduate school at age 28 and is now in medical school—with the full support of her husband. My younger daughter, having worked with human rights organizations for four years after college, entered law school at age 27. I am thrilled that they and their generation of women have opportunities to develop their full talents, but, more important, I am proud that they take advantage of those opportunities.

Although some job markets remain tight, those who obtain graduate degrees usually find good jobs and can command higher salaries. *Ms.* magazine reported that the salaries of women with master's degrees were significantly higher than those with undergraduate degrees, particularly among African-American women.[11] And graduate-school debts can be repaid with the increased salary.

Looking to the Future: Career and/or Family

When they look into the future, mothers still fret about and single daughters still struggle with finding the best way to achieve both a work and a family identity. Daughters are not as willing to sacrifice their personal lives for the sake of a career, as many women a decade before them were. They have witnessed women in their early forties who passed up childbearing to succeed in business. The younger women will not follow their example. They want it all—success and family.

A few years ago I interviewed therapists for an article I was writing and asked them what were the presenting problems of young career women. At that time many patients were troubled because they sensed their mothers did not accept their career plans and their delay of family. Yet they hesitated to talk with them because they feared that their mothers would confirm their suspicions. Their mothers only broached the subject through innuendo, leaving daughters in a quandary. A sense of dissatisfaction with each other prevailed.

But now, mothers' and daughters' ideas seem to be converging. Most mothers are proud of their daughters' career path and accept the fact that their daughters may be part of a two-income family and delay having a family. And daughters are more willing now than a decade or so ago to consider raising a family along with having a career. Their goals of balancing both parts of their lives are the same.

"It doesn't occur to me that I couldn't do both," said Francie, age 27. "I think during the eighties there was such an emphasis on women and careers that it colored my view for a while of being able to have children and a career."

Some young women were affected by the rhetoric of the eighties and thought they had to choose between a career and family. But as they grow older, they question that premise. "I do want a partner who will share my life," said a young professional. "I used to say emphatically no to the idea of kids, but now I think it would be nice to have kids." She has a serious boyfriend and says that she now is positive she wants children. She hasn't told her mother because it would be admitting that her mother was right all along. When she was 20, she told her mother she wanted a hysterectomy because she was never going to have children. Her mother calmly told her that some day she would meet a nice man and change her mind. Her mother was right.

Some daughters whose mothers worked continually when they were young do not question combining family and career. "It never occurred to me to take off work when I have children. That is not an option for me. My mom was always around although she worked full-time, and I assume I will be doing the same thing," said a 27-year-old graduate student.

Because these single women are not pushed to make a choice between career and family now, they visualize scenarios that would allow them to have the best of both worlds. Whether they remain at an office (choosing one with good day care), marry a partner who will work from the home and share responsibility for children, or work from home themselves, they seem confident that some scenario will work out. But they also show respect for any woman who chooses to stay home. They think the difference between their generation and their mothers' is that daughters have the choice to work or stay home while many of their mothers did not.

"We live in a society," said Jean, "that we can do anything we want, and if you want to be a mother, be true to that. Don't cut yourself off. If you want to stay home with your kids, that's okay. Be true to yourself and follow what you really want to do."

When I asked a young woman who was graduating from business school what advice she would give to mothers, she said: "Realize your kids weren't born to be copycats of you. You can't help but want your kids to emulate the values you hold dear, but I would recognize that they are unique individuals, not just there to fulfill your dreams and wishes."

Each generation of women contributes to the succeeding generation not only the gene pool but the values around which a family is based. A woman now has the freedom to move in and out of a work environment, taking time out for family and then reentering at a later stage. She also is free to remain in her field and search for good child care, or stay out of her profession until her children are grown. Whichever decision a daughter makes, her mother should honor her choice and help her in whatever way she can.

In 1991, Nike ran an ad for women's athletic shoes with the headline "You Do Not Have to Be Like Your Mother." I first noticed the ad because I was talking with many adolescent girls who voiced that sentiment. But as I listened to young-adult women, past the adolescent rebellious stage, I thought back to the ad which I had filed. I reread its message: "You do not have to be like your mother unless she is who you want to be. You do not have to be your mother's mother, or even your grand-mother's mother on your father's side. You may inherit their chins or their hips or their eyes, but you are not destined to become the women who came before you, you are not destined to live their lives. So if you inherit something, inherit their strength. If you inherit something, inherit their resilience. Because the only person you are destined to become is the person you decide to be.[12]

"Resilience and strength" are two characteristics that can bond two generations. As young women enter their midtwenties and rethink many of their options, they know their lives and their mothers' lives will differ. They also realize that they will intersect at many levels. As mothers and daughters share "strength and resilience" and appreciate each other's uniqueness, the bond between them strengthens.

7

Daughters of Divorce

Daughters
> *A Changing Relationship with Mother*
> *Father's Role*
> *Adjusting to Mother's Single Life*
> *Warming Up to a Stepfather*
> *Lessons They Have Learned*
> *Marriage Aspirations*

Mothers
> *Reinventing Herself*
> *Mutual Respect*

"We are the first generation who comes from a lot of divorce, and I wonder how that will affect us, how we will view the world," said Laurie as we were discussing her family and friends. Laurie is not the only one who ponders this question. Starting in the sixties, the annual rate of divorce rose sharply and peaked in 1979. Although the rate has declined slightly, the number of divorces remains far above the level of the sixties.[1] The daughters of these divorces are now young adults, perhaps contemplating marriage themselves, and the question remains: How do they view the world?

"None of my friends' parents were divorced," said a 55-year-old mother of a 27-year-old. "When I was young, if a father wasn't around, it was because he died." And she is right; not many mothers are daughters of divorce. The earliest data about divorce in the United States date back to 1860, but not until the midseventies did divorce exceed death as the cause of the dissolution of marriage in the United States.[2]

Contrary to speculation, however, marriage did not die. Over 65 percent of divorced women remarry.[3] And an estimated 60 percent of persons who married for a second time in the eighties had lived with someone before their second marriage.[4] So a young woman in her twenties or early thirties may have observed her mother during marriage to her father, through her single life, during cohabitation with a boyfriend, and in a remarriage to a stepfather. Are her life views different because of her parents' marital background? What effect does her mother and father's divorce have upon her as she enters the age of marriage? How does a mother who grew up in an intact family connect with a daughter she may have raised alone?

Daughters

A Changing Relationship with Mother

The anger and hurt from a parent's divorce are ameliorated or viewed in perspective during young adulthood as a daughter herself enters relationships and realizes the complexity of love. However, as daughters talk about their parents' divorce, the memories are fresh and the confusion of those years has left a mark.

"My parents got divorced when I was a very impressionable age, so I had no illusions that my life was going to be great. You just do what you can do to make yourself happy," said Edy and then she added, "as long as you're not doing it at someone else's expense." Edy was 13, indeed, a very impressionable age, when her parents divorced and her father moved in with another woman.

Many parents divorce during those sensitive years when a girl is awakening to her own sexuality and is conscious of her parents' intimate interactions. She is aware of the hugs, the laughs, the open display of affection, and the periods of anger. She watches how they treat each other and how they cope with family differences. Often when parents divorce during a daughter's adolescence, the normal tug of war that exists between mothers and daughters is altered. Daughters stop their constant criticism of their mothers, usually side with them, and comfort them, developing an emotional attachment that can reverse a daughter's normal adolescent withdrawal from her mother.

But a divorce disturbs daughters at any age. As a 30-year-old woman told her parents when they informed her that they were splitting, "How dare you wreck my home life, even though it's not my home anymore."

Another young woman tried to describe how a parent–child relationship changes after a divorce. "When you see your mom cry, you really form a very different relationship. When parents are still together, they are a united front, and you are still the child, no matter how old you are. But when that breaks down, you can move up a rung to be more of a friend with your mom."

Another woman whose parents had separated many times and finally divorced, phrased it a different way: "You become the comforter to your own mom. You see her vulnerability, but it allows you to form sort of a more adult relationship with her."

The years immediately following a divorce are the most difficult, demanding adjustment by all members of the family. A recent study compared psychological stress between divorced and married mothers. For divorced mothers, the number of stressful events and the accompanying depressive symptoms increased significantly after a divorce but diminished over the next three years.[5]

A daughter notices and worries about her mother's sadness or anger. "She had always been a lot of fun to be around, and it was the first time that she wasn't," Edy continued. "She still tried to put on a really good face for us. She would confide her troubles, and I felt she was more of a girlfriend. Unfortunately her authority broke down a bit because I knew that I could get away with more, but I tried not to take too much advantage."

Judith Wallerstein in her study of divorced families found that most girls become sympathetic helpmates to their mothers during and after a divorce.[6] Daughters have witnessed their mothers' transformation after divorce, observed their struggle with finances, loss of social life, and, sometimes, isolation from relatives. Mothers may not think their daughters are sensitive to their situation, but daughters study them and note their disadvantages and are proud of their achievements.

"My mom had to reinvent herself after the divorce," Cindy said as she described how her mother had to support herself, Cindy, and her sister. They moved into a small apartment, and her mother began temping, ending up working for the temp agency. "I've seen my mother deal with situations where she's gotten screwed. People have taken advantage of her, and she's had to become a different person, develop different strengths. I don't want to have to be in that position. I don't want to be alone in the world, but if I am alone I want to be able to know that no one's going to take advantage of me."

The theme of not being taken advantage of echoes through conversations with daughters of divorce. They don't want to be hurt as their mothers were, and they want to protect themselves "just in case." Whether the mother or father initiated the divorce does not seem to make a difference in young women's need to protect themselves from the unpredictable. They can't quite trust the promise of "happily ever after."

A mother and daughter often grow closer after a divorce especially if a mother has no one else to confide in. A daughter will listen, not let her down, and takes pride in the fact her mother has emerged, often a stronger person, from a divorce. In some cases, however, a daughter seeks out her father because she is afraid of losing him.

Father's Role

I interviewed many adolescent girls when I wrote *"Don't Stop Loving Me": A Reassuring Guide for Mothers of Adolescent Daughters,* and I know that fathers have a special place in a girl's life. Even sophisticated 18-year-olds told me they liked thinking of themselves as "Daddy's little girl" and appreciated his protective attitude. With older daughters, the same sense of specialness marks the relationship, even if a father has left the family. However, these adult daughters view their fathers realistically, acknowledging their faults and understanding why their mothers, in some instances, could not tolerate their husbands' behavior. But they do not want to lose a father. As adults, they can talk with their fathers more easily and often grow closer to them, but they remain conscious of the hurt that was inflicted on the family.

"My mom kicked my dad out cause he was fooling around, so he moved in with this woman," said Sis, who at an early age learned how to handle her father. "When I moved in with my first boyfriend, he hit the roof. I told him he was my role model, and where did he think I learned it. When he told me that was different, I just said, 'Keep telling yourself that.' "

Dad can become a scapegoat, blamed for everything that went wrong, and frequently is left out of the family circle, but a daughter can turn him around, forcing him to remember his family. Sis has insisted that her parents get together for her sake (and convenience). She and her boyfriend used to spend their holidays alternating between her mother's and father's homes, but then Sis told her parents that if they wanted to see her they would have to have some holiday meals together. And now her mother, her mother's boyfriend, her father and his new wife, Sis and her boyfriend celebrate together. Sis does not hesitate to tell her father what she thinks, but she said she could not speak out when she was younger: "When I stopped caring about what my dad thought, I could start accepting him. I grew up a lot quicker because of the divorce."

Money is a thorny subject when a young woman needs money for college and Dad holds the purse strings. "I had to beg my father for money every month," said one graduate (as did many). "I would have to wheedle and cajole. I hated it. As soon as I didn't have to take his money, I could grow up." The issue of college payment has been studied by researchers, who found that children of divorce are less likely to apply for college and less likely to enroll if accepted.[7] "It is well documented that children from disrupted families acquire less education," commented one of the researchers. A tightfisted approach to a daughter's education can unsettle even further the fragile postdivorce relationship between a mother and a father. Their opinions may differ about the type of college (public or private) and the means of payment. Schools weigh salaries of both parents, even if one parent is not contributing to the college support, so children of divorce often find themselves unable to obtain financial aid even when they need it.

Aside from money, daughters gravitate to their fathers for numerous reasons. One young woman went to live with her father because she could not tolerate her mother's new boyfriend, who had moved in two weeks after her mother "threw" her father out of the house. She thought her mother was acting like a "slut." Now, seven years later, she loves and understands her mother, spends a couple of nights a week at her house, and blames her father's lack of communication for her mother's falling in love with someone else. However, she thinks that she is better off living with her father and praises him for his other qualities. She asserts that she and her mother get along much better when they only see each other for short periods of time.

Even if they live at a distance, fathers remain an important influence in young adults' lives. A study of adult children conducted by a noted researcher of family relations found that the closer adult daughters feel to their fathers, regardless of the marital status of the parents or the quality of the daughters' relationship with their mothers, the happier, more satisfied, and less distressed they are.[8] Knowing that a father, regardless of his residence, cares and will keep in contact reassures a young woman of her status in the family. She is loved by both mother and father.

I was struck by the intensity of these daughters' feelings for their fathers, as though their own strong emotions would hold the bond together for the two of them.

"I need to preserve my relationship with my father," one young woman told me. "My mother wants me to hate my father, but whenever she starts talking about him, I tune out. He was my parent. My mom was depressed, and I remember her sleeping all the time. My dad was very involved with me." Although she and her mother seldom argue, she constantly argues with her father ("we're both volatile") but defends him because he was a dad to her. She did not learn until she was an adult that her father had physically abused her mother. She now understands her mother's depression but, in spite of the knowledge of her father's behavior, remains devoted to him. She says he never hurt his children and paid attention to her while her mother did not.

A frequent refrain in conversations with young women about their divorced fathers was, "We've gotten closer in the last few years." Often fathers have not been the custodial parent, and the ties may have slackened. But by the time their daughters reach young adulthood, fathers seem to take a renewed interest. The college bills no longer present a financial burden or a constant subject of discussion, and fathers often take pride in their daughters and enjoy spending time with them and their friends.

Some daughters side with their fathers during a divorce, but because they are living with mothers, they remain quiet. A 30-year-old woman told me her story: "My dad just walked out after 25 years of marriage, and my mom was really bitter and would say bad things about him. I couldn't deal with that, and my dad would never say anything negative about her. So I more or less sided with him; not outwardly, but deep inside I was thinking he has the courage to say this isn't working, so let's just end it, rather than living together unhappily. I kind of regret that I wasn't there enough for my mom, but I'm closer to my dad because he's more open. We talk about a lot of things."

Another daughter whose father has kept in close and continual touch with his daughters (even turning down a better job in order to stay in the same community) spoke of her admiration of her father. Even though he initiated the divorce, he did not want to divorce himself from his children and told them of his commitment. Now his daughter is in her midtwenties, spends as much time with her father and stepmother as with her mother and her boyfriend, and visits amicably in both homes. Post-divorce cooperation between a mother and father works best for daughters in these circumstances. It allows a daughter to accept and love her expanded family without fear of making one parent envious of the other. When both parties collaborate for the good of the children (even if they are adults), daughters are better able to face their futures with confidence.

Adjusting to Mother's Single Life

Another major adjustment for a daughter and mother is the acknowledgement of their similar roles as single eligible women. When daughter and mother both are dating, an awkward situation can exist that requires time for adjustment. Sometime an inappropriate role reversal takes place when a mother who feels out of touch with the dating game wants her daughter to coach her. "My mother started asking me about condoms and vaginal condoms and dental dams, and I said, 'Mom, let me get you some pamphlets!' A gynecologist had told her she didn't have to worry about AIDS, and her boyfriend was telling her the same thing, and I'm telling her that she has to take precautions." This

28-year-old daughter is not comfortable giving her mother sexual advice and thinks her mother tells her too much. But she listens because she knows her mother only has her.

Most young women don't want to talk to their mothers about sexual matters, and they certainly don't want to hear their mothers' problems. It may be tempting for single mothers who feel unsure of themselves to violate the fragile mother-daughter boundaries, but they must respect their daughters and always remain conscious of those boundaries.

When I asked another young woman if her mother objected to her living with her boyfriend, she laughed and said that her mother had brought different boyfriends when she visited (they live in different states) and they had slept together, so her mother couldn't complain about her boyfriend. But she acknowledged that she is not comfortable with her mother bringing boyfriends for visits and wished they would stay in a hotel. Again, this mother is insensitive to her daughter's feelings and violates the boundaries of their relationship.

Adjusting to a mother's social life and perhaps her eventual remarriage is not easy for a single daughter. She would like to concentrate on her own love life, not her mother's. "My mom and I started dating at the same time; it was weird," said one woman. "I thought all of her boyfriends were terrible, real controlling, and I tried to sabotage them." Another woman claimed that right after the divorce, she and her mother were a "team," but now her mother seems to "throw me over for a man at the slightest provocation." She knows her mother seeks a new life for herself and she doesn't complain to her mother, but she wonders why her mother depends on men so much, why she needs someone all the time. "The men in her life have to come first," she said.

When mother and daughter find themselves in the same single status, the mother-daughter boundaries may blur. But when a mother remarries, her single daughter steps aside and assumes still another role. She no longer feels as obligated to assist her mother since now her mother has a partner, but now she must adjust to being a stepdaughter to her mother's new husband.

Warming Up to a Stepfather

Because most young women live away from their mothers and do not have to reside with their stepfathers, they seem relieved that their moms have found mates. They now accept stepfathers more easily than they could have as teenagers. Often their attitude is "If he makes my mom happy, it's okay."

"I definitely sided with my dad in the beginning. I was angry and hurt and completely irrational," said a woman whose mother had left her father for another man, now her stepfather. "But because Mom was so patient, I came around and realized there are two sides to a story. Yeah, my dad was hurt, but my mom was hurt too. I had to live with my mother and her new husband for a summer, and that forced me to deal with the situation. I even call him Dad now, and he and my mom are like teenagers in love, so I'm happy for her."

Another woman who originally was more sympathetic to her father than her mother and disliked her stepfather also has warmed up to him. She talked about her stepfather belonging to an "older generation" who can't grasp the concept that women possess as much intelligence and ability as men, but she admitted that he is a "fun-loving guy and we have a great extended family that is fun to go home to. Mom's happy with her life, for what it is. I'm not sure if there's anything else that she's wishing that she had. She's kind of accepted it the way it is."

Her mother's contentment assuages her daughter and makes it easier for her to embrace her mother's new life and new husband. Her mother seems happy; that's all that counts.

Lessons They Have Learned

After their parents divorce, daughters frequently learn that their mothers possess enormous courage and fortitude to rebuild their lives. They also learn what to avoid in their own relationships. Some become extra vigilant about their choices of a man and often fear abandonment by a potential mate. Others determine to communicate better than their parents and not follow a particular parent's pattern of behavior. They all learn that they must be ready to provide their own financial security.

"My image of marriage has been distorted," said Trish. "My dad's been married three times, and my mom remarried someone who's been married three times. I don't want to deal with something like that, so I'll be very careful. I have an element of wariness."

Because divorce is so common in the United States, an "element of wariness" pervades the conversations of many young women, but that wariness is particularly apparent in those who have experienced the breakup of their families. Trish's family may represent one extreme of marriage, divorce, remarriage, divorce, remarriage. However, divorce rates for remarriages do not differ substantially from divorce rates for first marriages, and divorce rates during the first few years of remarriage tend to be higher than those of first marriages.[9] So Trish's situation may not be as exceptional as it seems at first glance.

Trish has adapted well to her family's situation, but when she talks about marriage for herself, she is cautious and says that communication is going to be her biggest challenge. She has learned that not communicating can lead to divorce, and she searches for someone who is willing to open up.

Sophie also has learned that lack of communication can ruin a marriage. She was 15 when her parents divorced and now observes her father with his girlfriend and her mother with her boyfriend. She told me she now "understand[s] where things can go wrong and what can happen if you let a certain thing bother you and let it go and go and go. You're going to flip out, not think rationally about it, and break. When you can't talk about it, it's like, 'Leave, get out of the house.' "

Sophie has a serious boyfriend and says they talk over almost everything. She doesn't think you can "overcommunicate." "I want him to listen and respond. I say to him, 'If I'm having sex with you and I'm going on birth control for you, then you are going to care.' "

Many young women share Sophie's passion for communication, which on the one hand is admirable and leads to deeper understanding between couples and, on the other, can be demanding and exhausting. A daughter's desire not to fall into the same patterns as her parents sometimes leads her to an oversimplification of her parents' problems. When a young woman's primary conversation with her boyfriend is about their relationship, something is wrong. Talking alone does not alter a problematic relationship. Mutual love and respect are built day to day, shaped by sharing interests and by generously and lovingly interacting, not solely on the ability to articulate hurts. When couples communicate well, they are talking about the events, people, and interests that intrigue them, and they enjoy sharing those feelings and opinions with each other. When one concentrates on what a partner does that is annoying or painful, communication breaks down. No one, not even a husband or boyfriend, likes attention focused on faults. Good communication includes more than discussing a relationship.

Rather than oversimplifying their parents' problems, some daughters can pinpoint precise patterns in their parents' marriage that caused disruption and unhappiness, an analysis that helps in their own relationships. Georgie reflected on her relationship with her boyfriend, Andy: "I have to stop myself because I find myself trying to make Andy feel guilty because that's what my mother did to my father. Sometimes I'll find myself saying things, and I'll wonder, Where the hell did that come from? I've absorbed those patterns, and I have to work really hard to get away from that because I hate myself when I do that."

Georgie's outlook is more realistic than Sophie's because she has selected a specific pattern of behavior that she does not want to emulate. Not having a model of a good marriage to follow, she is trying to create her own. She knows what behavior doesn't work, but does she know what behavior does work?

When researchers looked at the increased risk of children of divorced parents to divorce themselves ("intergenerational transmission of divorce"), they examined many factors: age at marriage, cohabitation, education, income, wife's employment, attitudes toward divorce, and interpersonal behavior problems. They concluded that "parental divorce elevates the risk of off-spring divorce by increasing the likelihood that offspring exhibit behaviors that interfere with the maintenance of mutually rewarding intimate relationships."[10]

These daughters have observed behaviors from mother or father (or both) that undermine the other person and lead away from mutuality rather than toward it. The pervasive fear that all children have of repeating the mistakes of their parents rests heavily on daughters (and sons) of divorce. "Whatever they did, I don't want to do it," commented one woman. Georgie is sensitive to her mother and father's interactions and realizes that she jeopardizes her relationship with her boyfriend when she falls into her mother's habit of using guilt trips as a tool. Many of her friends' parents are divorced, so she has searched for a family on which to model her behavior. She thinks she has found one in her boyfriend's family. Because her boyfriend has grown up in a family where there is mutual love between husband and wife, he understands and can tease when she lapses into "mom-talk."

Besides being aware of the modes of communication and parental behavior that they don't want to repeat, young women also feel a sense of insecurity. Many of them reach out for friends,

financial security, and activities to protect them from disappointment. A woman who was adopted at birth and whose adoptive
parents divorced felt particularly vulnerable: "I know life is just a
bubble and it's so easy to break it, and I want to make sure, if it
breaks for me, I have all this other stuff to make a complete life."

Judith Wallerstein, in her ten-year study of children of
divorce, found that girls often have a delayed reaction to their
parents' divorce. Because their mothers need them, they put
their own needs on hold, but ten years after a divorce, Wallerstein observed a "sleeper effect," comprising anxiety about relationships and fear of abandonment.[11] Alice, a 29-year-old
professional woman whose parents were divorced when she was
9, avoids the problem of abandonment by leaving people before
they leave her or by forcing people to leave her. "I think I do it
on purpose to speed whatever end is going to happen," she said.
"If I know when I'm going to be hurt, I'm okay. At least I have
control of it. If I'm unsure, I always try to force the worst thing
to happen." Alice is so afraid that any man who likes her, maybe
loves her, will eventually leave that she takes the first step to
ensure that he does leave.

Although these young women often understand the reasons
for their parents' divorce, they still fear their own failure. They
hope that by not following their parents' example, no matter
how vaguely or specifically they perceive their parents' reasons
for divorce, they will secure better relationships.

Marriage Aspirations

A parental divorce does not lessen a young woman's desire to
marry. When college students were interviewed about their marriage aspirations, those who perceived their parents' marriage as
unhappy preferred getting married at a later age, but the quality
of the parents' marriage was unrelated to their desire to get married.[12] This yearning for a strong, happy marriage is shared by a

mother and daughter, no matter what their ages. The number of remarriages attests to the durability of the institution of marriage.

The expectations of the dynamics within a marriage may change, however. Another study found that most women, but especially daughters of divorce, prefer a "companionship" marriage over a "traditional" marriage.[13] In a companionship marriage, each partner shares financial responsibilities, housework, care of the children, and decision making. In a traditional marriage, the husband provides the primary source of income while the wife has primary responsibility for the children and home.

This vision of a companionship marriage was voiced by many young women who cohabitate. Fair distribution of housework seems to be the big issue with many unmarried couples, even though they live with "enlightened males" and share financial and other responsibilities. "I know my boyfriend's not a sexist brute," said one woman whose divorced parents had a traditional marriage. "He just doesn't like to clean." She laughed as she said, "He says he hears his mom's voice whenever I ask him to clean. It's really frustrating because I don't want to fall into the mom pattern and I'm glad he's expressing how he feels, so I end up mopping the floor. I'll do more rather than nag, so instead I walk around slamming doors."

Whether a marriage is companionship or traditional, an estimated 89 percent of women born in 1970 will marry (as compared with 97 percent of women born between 1928 and 1932 and 95 percent of those born between 1948 and 1950).[14] Most young women, whether daughters of divorced or intact families, want to experience marriage.

Mothers

Reinventing Herself

When a mother "reinvents" her life after a divorce, her children are very much on her mind. She knows the divorce will affect her daughter but hopes the effects will be beneficial, especially if she has instigated the divorce. She wants her daughter to realize that one does not have to remain in an unsatisfactory relationship. "I took back my own name, got divorced, and left my children," Sharon said. "I was literally suffocating to death and had ten years of pain and anger. I thought I would die if I continued in the marriage. Both my children have said to me that the gift I gave them was to let them know that if you didn't like something in life, you can change it."

Most women have not left their children as Sharon did, but many women resemble her because, after divorce, they begin new careers, often remarry, as did Sharon, and consider themselves role models for their daughters.

Women who did not want a divorce and were unprepared for single parenthood take longer to recover. When divorced women eventually recover, they are grateful to their daughters who have comforted them along the way. "I want my daughters to be proud of me," said a woman who had experienced a very difficult divorce and was determined not to be a burden on her daughters. "I think my daughters see me as a role model. I've been more important to them because of their father leaving. I've been their central rock parent." Each daughter did not react in the same helpful way to her divorce. She describes one daughter as being her most trying relationship, but she works hard at maintaining a strong bond with her.

One mother who has not remarried rightfully takes credit for her successful children: "My daughters are happy and productive, and they feel good about themselves, and it makes me feel as though I did it right. I didn't disappear for weekends with men. I kept trying to keep everything normal. I'm very optimistic. They have good heads on their shoulders."

These mothers don't regret their unhappy marriages because they love the children who were born during that union. Many had married when they were young. "Perhaps if I had slept with Frank, I never would have married him," confessed one mother.

Jinny has been married three times. "My daughters are my whole life," she said. "All I wanted was to give my girls a good father. I tried, so I don't begrudge myself as long as I tried." She admitted that she has been spectacularly unsuccessful in choosing men (her current husband is an alcoholic) and worries about her daughters' choices, particularly her oldest daughter, who has been involved with a boyfriend who constantly breaks her heart. That daughter has terminated two pregnancies with this boyfriend and causes Jinny endless worry. Jinny keeps warning her daughter not to follow her marital tracks, that she must find a good job with financial security and marry a good man. Unfortunately, her daughter seems to be following her mother's example rather than her words. The fear that their daughters will gravitate toward unreliable men can be a constant worry for mothers who have messed up their own personal lives. Jinny has good reason to worry.

Many divorced mothers, in spite of setbacks, build new and exciting lives, find careers that mesh with their experience, and develop a cadre of new friends. They are successful women.

One study, done at the University of Wisconsin in Madison, looked at graduates from the class of 1957 (most were 52 or 53 years old when they were interviewed) and tested them on a number of psychological measures. On some psychological measures, such as openness to new experiences and higher levels of personal growth, divorced or separated women scored better than married women.[15] When divorced mothers apply themselves to new experience and personal growth, they and their daughters will benefit. This effort, as difficult as it may be for many women, will bring substantial psychological rewards. A daughter will recognize in her mother a female strength that she also can bring forth when she needs it.

Daughters, because of their mothers' divorce, may be anxious about their own chances of happiness, but their mothers' lack of marital success does not have to interfere with their love, appreciation, and, often, admiration of their mothers.

Mutual Respect

The closeness that mothers and daughters have developed during the difficult years of divorce and single life becomes apparent when young women talk about their mothers. Daughters appreciate their mothers' efforts to preserve family traditions and rituals, to maintain close contacts with all members of the family, and to create new lives for themselves. Especially as daughters enter adulthood and look at their own relationships with a view toward marriage, they often marvel at what their mothers have accomplished.

"My mom's a very strong woman and very assured. She's strong in the community [she is a physician] and in the family," said a 23-year-old whose father had just remarried. "It hasn't been easy for her, a lot of hard knocks that I never noticed until this year. I've come to appreciate her so much and understand her as a whole person so much more. Our relationship is stronger than it ever has been."

Beth, age 28, described her mother as a role model: "I always think back to my mom because of what she went through raising us kids. I can think logically about a lot of things, and I owe that to her. She has a very strong work ethic and strong values, and I look to that. She did everything by herself, and we all turned out well. It's pretty amazing."

The question asked by Laurie at the beginning of this

chapter—how do daughters of divorce view the world?—cannot be fully answered until young-adult daughters become the parents of the next generation. They still are processing their experiences through the lenses of young, uncommitted women. Their generation is the first to have lived with so many divorced parents. So far, their marriage aspirations and love of their mothers are similar to other daughters'. And as they enter into marriage, they will strive to achieve what their parents did not, but they will always be grateful that their mothers worked hard to sustain them during difficult times. The mother-daughter connection can remain strong and grow through both stress and contentment. Daughters are proud of their mothers, especially when they themselves, the daughters of divorce, are happy. As Beth said, "It's pretty amazing."

8

Three Generations:
Daughters and Mothers Talk
About Grandmothers

L eaf through any recent book on older women, and "grand-parenting" can scarcely be found in the index. Not only are grandmothers excluded from current literature about older women, they usually are left out of any discussion on women's development. Yet one generation of women impacts the next, and the reverberations of a loving or distant relationship are transmitted from grandmother to mother to daughter.

Daughters

Grandmothers of young women can claim a unique place in history. Their lifetimes have borne witness to historic changes in women's roles, including political (and sometimes personal) battles for women's rights. Yet the wisdom that springs from that experience is seldom sought, nor are grandmothers often asked by their 20- to 30-year-old granddaughters to share their history. Lack of proximity contributes to the problem. When grandmothers have moved away from families or families have moved away from them, the geographic distancing narrows the opportunities for a relationship. But physical distance alone need not close the door.

Some granddaughters are distanced or even blocked from truly knowing their grandmothers because of their own mothers' unhappy memories of childhood. This psychological distancing, more than geographic space, contributes to the divide and leaves a void for all three generations.

But for those granddaughters who develop a close bond with their grandmothers, no matter where they live, the mutual rewards are many.

"A Presence"

"I just love her presence," one young woman commented. "It's a comfort to know she's there." Although this grandmother-granddaughter pair have never lived in the same state, they write to each other, not weekly or even monthly, but often enough to feel a very special connection. They exchange telephone calls with equal infrequency because her grandmother seems to count the minutes on the phone, watching the dollars disappear as the minutes tick by. But the granddaughter understands her grandmother's discomfort with long phone calls and looks forward to longer and deeper conversations during their visits together. She can't visualize life without her grandmother. In spite of their brief exchanges, she relies on her grandmother's unconditional love and acceptance.

Granddaughters cherish any sign of their grandmothers' devotion. Letters merit special attention. (I still have the letters my grandmother sent to me when I was young, and my mother has continued the tradition of writing to my children.) Even grandmothers who just send postcards affirm that granddaughters are a special part of their lives. A young woman mentioned that she loves the "spirit of supportiveness" that she receives from her grandmother's letters. She shares them with her friends, and they all "love" her grandmother, even though they have not met her. Grandmothers, raised in an era when telephone calls were costly and faxes and E-mail were nonexistent, are often more comfortable and expressive in their writing. Although many granddaughters communicate with their mothers by E-mail, they are not inclined to E-mail their grandmothers. Grandmothers of the present generation of five-year-olds undoubtedly will.

Although geography may deny a grandmother's physical presence, her influence can still be felt. A young woman whose grandmother never lived close enough for them to spend much time together still remembers her advice—always telling her how important it was to go to college. She listened and went. At times when a mother can't sem to say anything right, a daughter listens to her grandmother. Her grandmother speaks without an agenda. Plus, she won't be hurt if her advice is ignored. A grandmother often feels more at ease in offering counsel to her granddaughter than to her daughter. A daughter is more inclined to hear her suggestions as criticism. A granddaughter takes her grandmother's suggestions less personally.

Sometimes all a granddaughter wants is a sympathetic listener. A grandmother can fill that role. "My grandmother was a compulsive listener," a man once told me. (Everyone who heard this was envious.) Although too few people can claim the distinction of being "compulsive listeners," an empathetic grandmother is deeply appreciated.

One 27-year-old, whose grandmother telephones her each week to hear about her work and romantic struggles, calls her the strongest woman she ever met. "My grandmother has a couple of master's degrees," she said, "and definitely was on the professional track. But in her time she couldn't have both family and profession, so she gave up a career. She identifies with me and bucks me up. She's a very neat woman because of her integrity and courage."

During times of crisis or despair, a grandmother, if she is willing, can put aside her own anguish at a family situation and comfort her granddaughter. When Annette's mother left her father for someone else, Annette was devastated. She didn't talk with her mother for months, but she could talk with her mother's parents. "When I was trying to figure out what the hell was going on with my family," Annette recalled, "my grandmother said, 'If your mom's unhappy let's figure out the key to her happiness, and if Joe is the key to her happiness we must look into that and see why she feels that way.' " Annette credits her grandmother for being "open to new situations" and helping her reconcile with her mother. Judith Wallerstein found in her study about the effects of divorce that although most grandparents lived far away and some feared getting "caught in the crossfire," those who reached out to their grandchildren received abundant gratitude and love in return.[1]

Granddaughters Reflect on Grandmothers

Grandmothers are remembered, even if they died a while ago. "My grandmother was my biggest influence," a 30-year-old woman told me. Her grandmother died when she was 18, but she remembers sharing with her the youthful dreams of becoming an outdoor specialist, a naturalist and explorer. Her grandmother listened and admired her, while her parents thought she was "crazy." Keeping her grandmother in mind, she followed her dream.

"My grandmother died when I was ten, but she taught me to cheat in every game I played," said another young woman with a laugh. She and her grandmother always made up the rules as they played, so she didn't realize she was cheating. However, recently someone observed her playing solitaire and pointed out that she was cheating herself. Her memories also include admiration for her grandmother's ability to cope with physical discomfort. During a weekend visit, she endured two heart attacks without mentioning them until she at last admitted she wasn't feeling well and was rushed to a hospital. While her granddaughter admired her grandmother's stoicism, she now realizes that it went too far—that one has to be sensible.

Grandmothers can teach their granddaughters through their example. Those who have observed their grandparents' long, successful marriages benefit from their grandmothers' experiences and advice. "My grandparents have been happily married for fifty-plus years and are very balanced about what the give-and-take of it is," said a young woman who was in the throes of deciding whether to marry her boyfriend. Her grandmother told her not to be naïve, that there was both the good and the bad times during a marriage, and, because marriage was such a "long road," that she should weigh her decision carefully. She treasured her grandmother's advice and decided not to head down the long road with her boyfriend.

A grandmother who is a pacesetter, who encourages her own daughters and her granddaughters to use all their talents, is particularly loved. One 26-year-old woman remembers her maternal grandmother giving her a book when she was very young. Although there were many, many children's books in her home as she was the youngest child, she never before had a book of her very own. How she loved the fable about a princess with two brothers. The father-king decided one day that his children had to grow up. He sent the two princes *and* the princess out on adventures. The princess saved a handsome prince in his castle and rode back to her father to tell him that she was going to marry the man she rescued. Years later the details of the revised version of the traditional fairy tale still are vivid. "I didn't realize until I was older," she said, "that my grandmother was a feminist." She knows her grandmother wanted her to hear the moral of this tale. Seek your own destiny. Choose your own prince.

If granddaughters are to fully appreciate their grandmothers, their grandmothers' life stories must be set in the historical context of the restrictions placed on women throughout most of the twentieth century. Women were expected to suppress their own talents, narrow their interests, and ignore the needs of the national or international community. Even if granddaughters have majored in history (or women's studies), they often cannot grasp the enormity of change brought about through the efforts of feminist women. Stories of their grandmothers' lives will lead to better understanding of generational differences.

Many grandmothers pursued their own interests in spite of the societal expectation that they stay within the confines of the home and concern themselves exclusively with family matters. Women who were in the forefront of women's rights, social reform, and racial integration stepped outside their traditional roles, and their stories also should be heard by their granddaughters.[2]

Mothers

Mediators of Intimacy

Young-adult daughters, in general, speak fondly of their mothers and laugh at their idiosyncrasies or their attempts (mostly in vain) to direct their lives. Many of their mothers, however, do not display that same open affection for and acceptance of their own mothers. And they can impact the relationship between granddaughter and grandmother. A grandmother may live far away or may have died, but the heartaches of a mother's uneasy relationship with her may run deep and influence a granddaughter's feelings toward her grandmother.

A solitary study about grandmothers and granddaughters examined the role of a mother as a "mediator of intimacy between grandmothers and their young adult granddaughters." Researchers found that when contact between a grandmother and her granddaughter is frequent, the relationship between them can be direct and not controlled by the mother. However, when contact is infrequent, a granddaughter is swayed by her mother's feelings.[3]

One young woman said she always thought of her grandmother (who died when she was a teenager) as sweet, good-natured, and kind, but her mother has told her that this grandmother was a high-maintenance person who caused more trouble in the family than anyone, especially her granddaughter, would imagine. Now she holds two images of her grandmother, her own and her mother's.

If a grandmother is still an active presence, her granddaughter notices how she is treated by her daughter, whether she is considered a joy or a burden or ignored. A granddaughter absorbs the interactions between the generations, watches the misunderstandings and the shared moments. She may wonder at times if the women's movement that promised to honor all women includes honoring the mother-daughter bond. She sometimes is confused by the conflicting messages she hears about her grandmother.

Rosie described her grandmother: "I have a wonderful image of this old woman who was very sweet and very independent and did a lot of things on her own because her husband was never around. She had a fabulous garden, was a horticulturist, and put a lot of energy into that." Rosie said her memories of her grandmother are really positive, but after she died, her mother told her that her grandmother drank too much and always had a glass of bourbon in the kitchen during the day. Rather than changing her memories of her grandmother, the information added another layer to her grandmother and explained some of her mother's complexities. Secrets affect later generations. Certainly her grandmother's drinking had repercussions throughout her mother's childhood.

As proud as grandmothers were with their husbands' and children's accomplishments, many were quietly frustrated at watching everyone succeed because of their tireless, behind-the-scene efforts, without being rewarded themselves. They believed they were nurturing their daughters' best qualities, their domestic abilities. But many daughters, now in their own mid-life, do not agree with their mothers' interpretation of their childhood or adolescent years together. They resent their mothers because they were not encouraged to be independent. Some complain that they were not educated as well as their brothers. They were trained for home only. But grandmothers thought they were doing the best they could.

Granddaughters also should hear these stories of mother-daughter misunderstandings so they can more fully comprehend why their mothers do not openly embrace their grandmothers. Whenever tales about life with grandmother are told, they should be related with affection for women who did not have the opportunities and community support that are available to their granddaughters.

"The Ghost of My Mother"

"The Envelope," a poem by Maxine Kumin, sent to me by my mother, beautifully portrays the generational transmission of "mother."

> It is true, Martin Heidegger, as you have written,
> *I fear to cease,* even knowing that at the hour,
> of my death my daughters will absorb me, even
> knowing they will carry me about forever
> inside them, an arrested fetus, even as I carry

the ghost of my mother under my naval, a nervy
little androgynous person, a miracle
folded in lotus position.
Like those old pear-shaped Russian dolls that open
at the middle to reveal another and another, down
in the pea-sized, irreducible minim,
may we carry our mothers forth in our bellies.
May we, borne onward by our daughters, ride
in the Envelope of Almost-Infinity,
that chain letter good for the next twenty-five
thousand days of their lives.[4]

A mother's "ghost" appeared continually during my conversations with mothers that were intended to focus on their daughters. It's a presence that may be soothing. "I like spending time
with my mom," said one 56-year-old woman who meets her
mother regularly. They enjoy each other's company and often
discuss their mutual love and concern for the granddaughters.

A grandmother can bring a balance to a mother's concerns
about her daughter by offering a longer-term outlook on a
problem that a mother thinks is immediate and disastrous. She
also can remind her daughter of her own turmoil during those
early adult years.

Georgina, whose mother died a couple of years ago at age 84,
describes her mother as a role model for her children. Other
women in the room acknowledged that Georgina's mother was a
role model for their children also. "She was elegant, so wonderful, and had a happy life," said Georgina. Her grandchildren
even listened to her comments about table manners (lessons
Georgina was not successful in conveying). Georgina and her
sister often talk about how they would love to have their
mother's advice now. When her sister's son was very ill, she

called Georgina and wept over the phone, "If only Mother were here, she'd know what to do." "That's the way we grew up," said Georgina. "Mother always knew just what to do." Georgina and her sister are very accomplished women. They have loving daughters and successful careers. Their mother encouraged them. She was proud of her daughters and her granddaughters. She was the head of an ideal grandmother-mother-granddaughter team.

Some "ghosts" of mother are not so soothing. A remark I hear frequently in workshops is that women don't want to parent their daughters the way they were parented. These women judge their relationships with their daughters against the background of their feelings about their own mothers. Women want friendships with daughters that they could not have with their mothers. And they want their daughters' lives to stand apart from theirs, as distinct and fulfilled. If these desires are in contrast to what they had, they fight their mothers' ghosts.

"She wants me to be someone other than I am," commented a woman in her fifties about her mother. She senses her mother's underlying dissatisfaction with her but cannot pinpoint the cause, as much as she's tried. At last, exhausted by the effort to please, she has decided just to be herself. She wants the next generation, her daughter, not to sense that same lack of approval. She wants her daughter to rest assured that she is satisfied with her. She compares her daughter's life with her own life and is keenly aware of the contrast between their friendship and her nonexistent friendship with her mother.

These women in their fifties bridge the generational changes in women's opportunities. They want their daughters to feel the security and orderliness of the fifties that their mothers gave them. But they also want their daughters to aspire to the opportunities and autonomy that came with the breakaway sixties and seventies. Most believe their daughters can do everything successfully—a feeling many did not receive from their mothers.

During one interview session, three women gathered to talk

about their daughters, and inevitably the conversation turned to their own mothers. Although these women knew each other rather well, each one revealed, much to their surprise, that her mother was an alcoholic. This was not the first time I had heard this type of revelation.

Women offered various explanations for their mothers' alcoholism. "My mother was never happy," Marcelle said. "She had cancer when I was 12 and was told she was going to die. She became a roaring alcoholic and didn't die until I was 29." Marcelle took over the responsibility for the household, raising her brothers, fixing the meals. Often she would find her mother drunk on the floor at three in the afternoon. Her mother felt she never fit into the small town where they lived. "She had a miserable life," admitted Marcelle. But in spite of the terrible times, Marcelle said that "love is what got me through those crazies. I always felt loved by both my mother and father." She recalled listening to an interview with Liza Minnelli, daughter of Judy Garland, who said that in spite of all the insanity of her mother's alcohol and drug years, she knew she was loved.

Many daughters, with heroic effort, surmount the difficulties that they faced as daughters of alcoholics. "My mother was mentally ill and tried to medicate herself with alcohol," said another woman. Although she had a "wretched" childhood, she took care of her mother after the latter became impaired in her seventies due to an alcohol-induced stroke. This woman shared the details of her childhood with her daughters, but she also showed them the strength of the mother–daughter bond. She never turned away from her mother and offered her support when she was in need.

Some women, in spite of not getting along with their mothers, are able to hold their tongues and allow their daughters to develop their own relationships with their grandmothers. "I respect my mother's life now that she's dead more than I did while I was dealing with our relationship," said one woman.

"She was jealous of everything I did, but had a great personality and my children had a wonderful relationship with her; they thought she was a terrific character."

"Jealous of everything I did" may be an underlying cause of some dissatisfaction in relationships between grandmothers and midlife daughters. When the social climate for women changed in the sixties and seventies, many grandmothers could not adjust. They envisioned their daughters emulating them, not marching in peace demonstrations, traveling on their own, thinking of their careers, or starting careers after they were married and had children. When their daughters opted for new choices, they were opposed. Some may have harbored jealousy and secretly wished they could participate. Some waited it out, persuaded by others that their daughters and their friends would outgrow this rebellious phase. It did not happen.

Most 50- to 60-year-old women did not go through a rebellious stage. When these women talk about their mothers, they often note that they did not have the same relationships with them as other family members did. This seems especially true when sisters span a space of time and the younger ones were caught in the societal upheavals of the late sixties and early seventies. "My mother would choose her words carefully and would not say things that would put me down," commented Nita, age 58. "My younger sister and she had more conflict. I was the oldest. I baby-sat and had good grades. I didn't make any waves; I never got into trouble."

Those who never made "waves," who were steadfast and traditional, who followed in their mothers' footsteps earned their mothers' gratitude. Others who wanted to make their own waves often created a monsoon, not only in families in the United States but around the world. Many of today's young women have mothers who migrated to the Unites States, creating a more complex grandmother-mother-daughter relationship.

A woman in her midfifties, who migrated twenty-five years

ago, told me that she made two major decisions when she lived in her native land. She decided to go to a professional school and then married outside her social class. Both choices distressed her traditional parents and tore apart the family structure. Her mother pleaded with her to change her mind, asking how they would ever explain her behavior to relatives. She suggested that her mother just tell everyone that her daughter was "out of control." Now she and her 22-year-old daughter visit her mother regularly in her native country. The trips have given her daughter a new appreciation of her mother's struggles and an insight into her family origins.

Others who wanted to step outside the well-defined boundaries of behavior received a similar message: Do not be independent. Some midlife women won't even say they received a "mixed" message. To them the message was clear: Don't change tradition. One 54-year-old had been promised a car in lieu of going to graduate school in another city—a local university would do, she was told. She didn't go away. Another was told that if she joined the peace corps, she would "break her mother's heart." She didn't join. "They just didn't want girls moving ahead or away," said one woman. "They weren't angry about it; they just didn't focus on me the way they did my brothers."

Some women were dissuaded from living in apartments on their own. When Molly told her mother she was going to get an apartment, her mother cried that she had been waiting, all through Molly's college years, for her to come home. When Molly obliged and moved back in with her mother, she was "miserable." It wasn't until she married that she moved out. Her mother's need to control is a lasting memory. She wishes she had established her independence earlier because the pattern of control continues to this day.

If a mother successfully keeps her daughter under her thumb—and her roof—while she is establishing herself during early adulthood, it is difficult for a young woman to develop

confidence in herself. For those, now in their fifties or early sixties, the pattern of being dominated by Mother is so entrenched
it is hard to change, even with an aged parent.

"My mother is very difficult. She expects me to call her every
day at five or else she can't have a good evening, so I make it
a point to be by a phone every day by five," complained a
53-year-old woman, relating one of a litany of unhappy experiences that began when she was young. When I asked her if she
and her mother had ever sought counseling, she replied, "She
would tell me that she didn't need it, but that I did." This woman
copes because her mother lives in a different state, but her
mother's dominating personality disturbs her daughter's tranquillity even from a distance of one thousand miles. She seems pow-
erless to speak up to her. "It's too late for her to change," she said.

The inability to confront, which began thirty years ago, is
now affecting three generations. Her daughters, both in their
twenties, don't want their grandmother joining them on vacations because she has ruined many good times. They sneak away
without telling her. What a shame this mother didn't confront
the issue of control years ago so that all the family could benefit
from an honest relationship in their adult years.

Understanding Grandmother

To progress from a hard-edged relationship into friendly and
happy communication takes insight as well as time and effort.
Rightly called the "sandwich" generation, women in midlife often must accommodate and empathize with both aging
mothers and young-adult daughters *and* assume the lead in establishing good communications with both.

When I talk with mothers of adolescents, I remind them that
the adult must always take the lead in changing a disturbing
situation. An adult with more experience and patience than an
adolescent can refrain from quick retorts as she struggles to listen

to her daughter's anger and unhappiness. A mother can bring calm to a relationship with an adolescent girl, but it requires effort, patience, and love.

Establishing good communication with a mother's mother, however, may require even more effort, patience, and love because it requires sublimating one's own needs as a child in the relationship. "She never tried one iota to understand me," complained a 59-year-old woman. Trying to change their relationship now when her mother is in her eighties seems impossible to her.

"Seek first to understand. Then to be understood," wrote Steve Covey, describing the habits of successful people.[5] If women want their mothers to understand them, they must first seek to understand them—and the first step is to listen.

It may seem unfair that a woman in midlife has the burden of righting the relationship if there are misunderstandings. Yet she often must take the first step if only because no one else will. With the perspective of knowing her mother will not live forever, a midlife woman may be willing to rethink old wounds and look for cues to open up new avenues of communication with her.

However, because the patterns of communication have been set for years, mother and daughter easily fall into their historically prescribed roles, and the transition to a friendlier relationship is difficult. Many older people become more entrenched in their habits and are not willing to budge. But it is a highly unusual grandmother who does not want to be more loved and accepted by relatives, especially by her daughter and granddaughters. If a grandmother thinks her attitude toward her daughter is disrupting her relationship with a granddaughter, she may be more willing to relax and reveal her fears. What most older people fear is that they will be ignored or considered useless or boring. Their personalities begin to reflect these fears, and their innate desire for love and attention is interpreted as interference, control, or domination. They want to be listened to, to be understood.

Just as young-adult women need to be heard, so do their grandmothers. A woman in midlife becomes a sounding board for two generations.

Transmission of "Feminine Energy"

When mothers talked about their own mothers, I was impressed with the stories that revealed these older women's strong characters. That strength may have been bridled by disappointment, lack of opportunity, or addiction, but it enabled them to weather family reversals, adapt to economic changes, recover from personal loss during war, and, often, adjust to brand-new countries. Just as I heard heroic stories of grandmothers, I heard exciting stories or enviable accomplishments of granddaughters, young women who have promising careers or have worked in third-world countries or have overcome cancer.

When I asked some mothers where they thought this strength, this "feminine energy," originated, Shirley responded that "it comes through the generations. I can look and see where my grandmother was and where my mother was, where I am and where my daughter is."

Shirley and her mother had a very difficult relationship, which Shirley decided to rectify. She arranged for them to meet for lunch at a point halfway between where they lived. Shirley, a lawyer, made herself available to meet regularly this way. Slowly, Shirley recalled, they unwound all the "stuff" that had kept them apart, causing friction, frustration, and confrontation through the years. About two years before her mother died, they had finished clearing up the past. "We were having the kind of conversations you have with your daughter." Her mother died quite suddenly, and Shirley still misses their telephone conversations. When it gets to be 10:30 P.M. she yearns to reach for the telephone.

Oftentimes what begins as a casual exchange unexpectedly adds a new dimension to the relationship. Shirley recalled giving her mother a book. The book was about women who wanted to write but set the desire aside and sublimated themselves to others. Her mother read it in an airport and "just sobbed and sobbed and sobbed and then called to tell me the story of my grandmother." Her mother's mother had been a writer but had to publish stories under a man's name. Somehow she managed to fit her writing in between making pies and washing diapers. "I think my mother also aspired to be a writer," Shirley said. "She always treasured what I had written. There was a part of her that valued what I did even while she always talked about her sons and what they were doing."

Eventually Shirley and her mother were able to talk about their past difficulties. "I dated a black guy in high school, and I think in many ways, Mom had always felt she stood in the way of that. [Shirley had gone on to a very unhappy marriage.] She said to me one day at lunch, 'Do you think it would have been different if . . . ?' " Shirley reassured her mother that her interference in her romance had been all right. "I have such a strong ego and sense of wanting to produce, and so does he, that we would have killed each other," she told her mother. She and her ex-boyfriend have remained friends and have acknowledged to each other that they would not have survived a marriage. Her mother was tremendously relieved to hear Shirley's interpretation. Shirley remembered coming away from that lunch thinking, "Wow, who would ever have thought we could have had that conversation." They even reached a point that they could discuss philosophical issues, topics dear to Shirley's heart. "My mother really struggled in later years with the question of evil, and we had lots of conversations about that. She had never thought there was evil, and she finally came to the place where she thought there was."

One of the wonderful elements of Shirley's relationship with her mother is that it went through many transformations: from anger to distance to acceptance and reevaluation and then at the end to mutual love and deep conversations about the meaning of life.

Shirley's daughter writes and edits small-edition books, a talent perhaps passed down from her great-grandmother—a history she might never have known if her mother had not decided to reach out to her own mother.

The Caretakers

"My maternal grandmother moved in with us eight years ago when she became sick," Bea, a 23-year-old said. The family, including her father, made the decision to bring her home rather than sending her to a nursing home. Her grandmother needed constant care, but her mother wanted to be the caretaker and refused to bring in outside help. Bea helped out when she could; because she lived at home during college, she frequently was available. Memories of her grandmother, who died recently, went beyond memories of sickbeds and difficult nursing. She remembered going to her grandmother's "huge garden and picking blueberries and raspberries and blackberries and helping her bake." Her grandmother lived close by, and the intimate moments they shared when she was in good health helped Bea and her mother through the difficult years of caring for her in poor health.

One in every four families are providing physical and emotional assistance to older relatives and friends—22.4 million households, which represents a threefold increase from a decade ago.[6] Seventy-two percent of the caretakers are women, 64 percent of them work part- or full-time, and 41 percent also are caring for children under the age of 18.

If the United States is returning to three-generation households, public and private agencies that support at-home care (like visiting nurses) need to be championed. Outside help is crucial in a situation where a grandparent is critically ill, her daughter is working and, in some cases, still raising their children.

So much the better if the grandmother–mother–daughter relationship is a good one. Recollections of happy times can ameliorate the tedious work of caring for a sick person and the anguish of watching a loved one suffer.

Coming Full Circle

All women desire a friendship with their mothers. It seems increasingly possible that these friendships will flower as "mommy-bashing" goes out of favor. The term *mommy-bashing* was used in the writings and heard in the discourse of many women through the seventies and eighties. It described their outrage at mothers who, they claimed, ruined their lives. Encouraged by therapists to reexamine their childhood relationship with their mothers, women found mothers a convenient dumping ground for their problems and frustrations. Mommy-bashing was especially prevalent among activist women. Mothers under attack were reluctant to attend therapy sessions with their daughters for they knew the sessions would focus on them, their faults and failings.

"Be careful of the therapists you recommend," a colleague warned me. "Many are trained to look exclusively at mothers as the main problem." Many therapists still direct women away from self-analysis and toward analysis of their mothers' faults. Mothers feel helpless under the subsequent bombardment.

No mothers are perfect, of course, and many mothers have attempted to control their daughters, dampen their dreams, and discourage their adventures. However, as a daughter becomes an adult and assumes responsibility for her own life, a mother's role as guide, good or bad, should fade. Sometimes a daughter, even in midlife, must clarify the boundaries. That discussion should take place as early as possible so they can enjoy each other without fear of control.

An adolescent goes through a natural stage of mommy-bashing. She withdraws from her mother and criticizes almost every aspect of her personality. Some may continue critiquing for a time into young adulthood. "Our children have decided to inform us of our failures as parents," wrote Jeanne Walker in the *New York Times* as she recounted how frequently her children regaled her with complaints about their upbringing.[7] They seemed intent on making her fully understand that she and her husband had been inadequate parents.

But most young women do not blame their mothers for their unhappiness and have outgrown the adolescent habit of criticizing their mothers. Did the mothers of the present generation of 20- to 30-year-olds parent better than their mothers did? Is that why they relate better?

Certainly mothers of 20- to 30-year-olds know more about female development than their mothers did, but comparing parenting styles of different generations is a futile exercise. Women, coming into adulthood at dissimilar sociological and economic times, will naturally look at themselves and their female offspring differently.

The young-adult women I interviewed genuinely like the other female members of their families—mothers and grandmothers. Perhaps their attitude comes from having more opportunities and outlets for their energies. Even beyond that, I think young women sincerely want to respect their mothers and grandmothers. They witness enough put-downs of women outside their homes and want to feel their mothers' and grandmothers' strength. They are more willing to try to understand the generational differences and not mommy-bash.

A study at Wellesley College reminds us that it is no longer unusual to find an 80-year-old mother who has a 55-year-old daughter who has a 30-year-old daughter who may have a

5-year-old daughter. The study found a strong link between the quality of an adult daughter's relationship to her mother and the daughter's psychological health.[8] Most women in the small study maintained "rewarding" relationships with their mothers and were able to talk over problems, enjoyed each other's company, got along smoothly with their mothers, and had mothers who helped out when needed. But the study also suggests that the fewer roles a woman has, the more "central to her mental health is her relationship with her mother."

If a daughter has a poor relationship with her mother and is not occupied with career or family or both, she may overly focus on her mother and be disturbed by what seems to be her mother's uncooperative personality or past parenting. An active life is good mental health for everyone, but especially important for daughters who don't feel loved or understood by their mothers, no matter what their age.

Although keeping communication flowing between three generations requires time and forethought, the establishment of three generations of friendship benefits all three women. It is a gift for all women and certainly a goal for the youngest generation of the trio. They want to maintain contact as long as they can. As one young woman put it, "I pray to God my grandmother will be here for my wedding." Although they may not be present in the psychological literature of our day, grandmothers are present in their granddaughters' lives.

9

Lesbian Daughters

Background

Daughters

Coming Out to Herself

Coming Out to Her Mother

Coming Out to Her Father

Redefining Herself

Mothers

Hearing the News

Telling Friends

Accepting a Daughter's Partners

Advice from Mothers and Daughters

When I interviewed mothers and daughters for my book *"Don't Stop Loving Me": A Reassuring Guide for Mothers of Adolescent Daughters,* neither mothers nor daughters talked about female homosexuality. Mothers with adolescent daughters who preferred jeans to skirts, girlfriends to boyfriends, who were outspoken, athletic, and aggressive knew that their daughters were acting like normal, energetic high-school girls. Mothers did not question their daughters' sexual orientation. They understood that girls' friends mean everything to them and that girls go through a natural phase of having crushes on women: teachers, coaches, scout leaders.

Girls attracted to women don't worry about being considered different. Their friends share their feelings. Girls enjoy physical affection with other girls, hugging, kissing, sharing beds with each other at slumber parties. Both mothers and daughters can recall being infatuated with certain teachers, following them down the school halls, and trying to learn about their personal lives. Nothing extraordinary about their behavior.

Mothers of sons, however, don't have that easy attitude about their sons' fascination with the same sex. They accept the rock stars or athletes who remain on posters in their bedrooms, but many are squeamish when a son spends a lot of time with a male teacher or coach or seldom hangs out with the "regular" guys. If a son has girl friends but not a girlfriend, a mother may urge him to start dating.

When I interviewed mothers for *Strong Mothers, Strong Sons: Raising the Next Generation of Men*, some mothers voiced apprehension about their sons' sexual orientation. These sons tended to be more artistic, less athletic, had friends who were girls, but were not interested in dating. Could he be gay? they wondered. The mothers who talked animatedly about their sons' girlfriends seemed relieved that their boys, indeed, were straight. Realizing that a son's sexual preference could present problems to their mothers, I included a chapter about gay sons in my book.

Because young women are more likely to acknowledge their homosexuality after adolescence (sometimes long after), I decided to include their voices in this book. Their "coming out" can dramatically and, often, adversely affect their relationship with their mothers. Therefore, I sought out young lesbian women to interview. Through personal interviews, telephone conversations, and E-mail, I talked with women who identified themselves as lesbians and who had come out to themselves and to their families when they were in their twenties.

I also interviewed straight mothers of lesbians in order to understand more clearly their relationships with their daughters, how they reacted to their daughters' coming out, and how their relationship has progressed since that time.

Background

More attention has been paid to male than to female homosexuality in psychological research. However, since the establishment of women's studies courses and the creation of a women's division of the American Psychological Association, research into the developmental markers of lesbians is increasing.

Lesbian identity is, in the words of noted researcher Laura S. Brown, a "self-ascribed definition held by a woman over time and across situations as having primary sexual, affectional, and relational ties to other women." Brown notes that a lesbian identity may not be "congruent with overt behavior at any point during the lifespan."[1] Brown's use of the word *self-ascribed* implies that a woman herself decides if she wants to be defined as lesbian. Women come out at various times in their lives.

Women who were attracted to boys during their teens or women who have enjoyed adult heterosexual relationships may not identify themselves as lesbians until later in life. The option of being a lesbian was unknown to them during adolescence, "not even on the menu," as one woman said. Some may have married out of fear of rejection or confusion about their orientation. They did not dare imagine a homosexual relationship, much less a committed relationship. They banished such thoughts and lived a heterosexual life.

But other women sense from the moment of their first sexual awakenings that they are lesbians and have no doubts as to their sexual orientation. They may not discuss their suspicions with anyone, but they feel their differences and vividly recall their early attractions to women. They are more likely to come out during their late teens or early twenties.

According to some studies, women who maintain a strong commitment and dedication to feminist issues may also choose to call themselves lesbians. And yet another group of women, those who could be identified by researchers as bisexual, may choose the lesbian identity.[2] Although the lesbian "category" is broad, the number of lesbians remains small, in comparison to gay men. Although researchers disagree about the numbers, a 1992 survey conducted by the University of Chicago estimated that 0.9 percent of women surveyed identified themselves as homosexuals and 0.5 percent identified themselves as bisexual.[3]

As in the studies of gay men, biological and psychosocial models of lesbian development are put forth. Some research suggests that lesbians are born with "irreversible" hormonal exposure which sets their course toward homosexuality (the biological model). In contrast, researchers who investigate psychological or social factors suggest that lesbians do not have an innate homosexual orientation but, for a variety of reasons, "choose" a lesbian identity.[4] Researchers on both sides of the often intense debate (biology-essentialists vs. psychosocial-social constructionists) have decided that no firm conclusions can be drawn about the development of homosexuality.[5]

Prospective studies that focus on sexual orientation and follow subjects from infancy to adulthood are nonexistent for women. A few retrospective studies that ask lesbians to reflect back on their lives can be found, but the studies are small and don't reflect the broad experiences of lesbian women. Personal stories must suffice.

Daughters

Coming Out to Herself

The most common marker of the lesbian experience is the process (not the onetime announcement) of coming out. The process is long. A woman must come out to herself first, by acknowledging that she is attracted to women, prefers women as sexual partners, and is able to call herself a *lesbian*. The word itself frightens women who have been brought up to think of homosexuality as deviant behavior or who have observed gay women and men being ridiculed or attacked. They fear that their families will reject them or throw them out of the house. They worry about their place in society. Will they be fired if the boss knows? If they have been successful in concealing their attraction to women, they wonder if they will lose their straight girlfriends. Will their guy friends turn aside? Will their lives ever be the same?

"I had no way of identifying myself as a homosexual, so I just denied it," commented Allyson. She lived in a small town where "no one was a lesbian." When she changed jobs and moved to a new city, she met a couple of coworkers who were open about their homosexuality. This exposure gave her the courage to admit to herself that she also was a lesbian. With great relief, she left her boyfriend and entered the lesbian world.

Usually, the first step in a lesbian's development is to question the normal (heterosexual) expectations for behavior and admit homosexual attractions. Allyson used the word *deny*. For years she wondered about her feelings toward her girlfriends, but because she could not meet or consult with other lesbians, she remained in limbo. A heterosexual woman may occasionally feel attracted to a woman but would not doubt her primary sexual attraction to men. If a heterosexual woman meets lesbians, she does not feel the same sense of relief and recognition that Allyson did.

The questioning of sexuality can begin at any age. Tish was 16 when she had her first lesbian experience. "[I was] very much in love and knew it was natural for me," she recalled. Raised in a Pentecostal religion, she thought that admitting she was a lesbian would mean accepting that she was corrupt, "of the devil and going to hell." So she continued to date males, even though she considered herself and her friend a "couple." She did not come out until she was 24.

Many lesbians don't allow themselves to act on their feelings for women until they are mature. Adolescence is a time of experimentation, and for some, that involves sexual experimentation.

Some psychologists believe that a person's sexual preference is not determined until after adolescence, that it is in flux during adolescence.

Although Tish, now 29, was able to date boys and have an affair with a girl at the same time, not many girls who wonder about their sexuality are willing to take that risk. Another woman told her former teammates during a high-school reunion that she was a lesbian. Some of them disclosed, much to her surprise, that they also were lesbians, suspected she was in high school, but were reluctant to inquire. She herself said that if these girls had tried to include her in their lesbian group during high school, she would have rejected them and been embarrassed if they even hinted that she was a lesbian.

"I was a junior in high school when I had my first sexual experience with a girl," reported Celena. "I had so little permission to explore it that I blocked that episode from my mind and kept the feelings underground."

Many affiliate with other lesbians for the first time when they are in college. The increased number of gay and lesbian organizations on campus offers them the opportunity to come out in a friendly environment. However, not all women found those organizations and many look back on their college years with sadness.

Celena said that when she went to college, she found an "underground network." She recalled it was like "a subculture in pain and self-loathing." The experience deeply disturbed her and again delayed the acceptance of herself as a lesbian. Not until a few years later when she entered graduate school did she permit herself to entertain the possibility of being a lesbian. When she met a particularly attractive lesbian graduate student, Celena "allowed" herself to come out and went into therapy to recover her self-confidence.

Most lesbians, after they have come out to themselves, seek

other lesbians and want to initiate relationships. At this point, most of these activities are concealed from their immediate families because they remain uncertain of their families' reactions.

Suzy dated men on and off and had many close male friends, intimate but not sexual. She described them as "great" but felt that something was missing. When she was 23 and vacationing with a male friend, she encountered an attractive woman who invited her for dinner. She knew intuitively that the request for dinner was a date. The woman had made an assumption that Suzy was a lesbian, even though Suzy had not admitted it to herself. Suzy recalls that she was very aware of what was happening and the night "blew" her away. But it was several months before it "sunk in" that they really were "dating." The woman took a risk, sensing that Suzy would respond. "It was so obvious," Suzy recalled, "all the tumblers clicked." In other words, all her self-doubts disappeared, and a lesbian partner felt right for her.

Coming Out to Her Mother

A network of lesbian friends usually gives a young woman the courage to come out to her family. Often she first divulges her "secret" to a sibling, who is more likely to be understanding and nonjudgmental. Many women report that their siblings were not surprised and perhaps knew them better than they knew themselves (or would admit they knew).

When Celena at last found the nerve to tell her mother, her mother (when she recovered from the shock), said, "I'm not going to be able to march for this." Celena assured her that she wouldn't have to and that she, herself, was not ready to march.

"I came out at age 20 to my mother," Jerrie said. "Since I've been little, I've wanted close and intimate friendship with girls and older women, not sexual. It just kind of grew. I was always passionately involved with girls. My first sexual feelings with a girl were at 19. I had boyfriends, but not the same intimacy or closeness. I always felt empty or hurt. I always went to the comfort of women friends."

Disclosing to mothers remains the hardest step and becomes the overriding concern. Lesbians exchange stories of how others did it, searching for advice on the best way. As Wendy Rosen wrote in her study of lesbians and their mothers, "Not all lesbians come out to their mothers, but with or without disclosure it is a preoccupying theme in the lives of most lesbians."[6] How to tell, when to tell—no time seems quite right. One young woman spent a week vacationing with her parents but couldn't figure out how to tell them. Instead, she went home and wrote them a letter. Some women take the opportunity of a family gathering to come out to their parents. Perhaps hoping that a large group would divert their parents' attention, two women I interviewed came out during a family funeral.

The agony of deciding if and when to tell their mothers can be intense. Young women have to prepare for their disclosure and address their own fears. When a study asked lesbians to list the concerns they had about disclosure, they named: "causing pain to and disappointing parents, rejection by parents, loss of love and approval, being seen as sick, causing conflict and disharmony with parents." A few even feared causing a parent's death. Some women thought their fathers would interpret lesbianism as a rejection of men, especially them, while others worried that their mothers would consider it a disapproval of their lives as married, heterosexual women.[7] Still others thought their mothers would blame themselves for their daughters' lesbianism, making it even harder to tell them.

Women recalled their mothers' various responses. One reacted immediately with "You don't expect me to tell my friends." Another mother exclaimed, "You know what I think of this and better yet what God thinks of this, but I want you to be happy and healthy." Some mothers were able to express their love and immediately responded, "I still love you." Some who suspected that their daughters were lesbians were relieved that the truth was out.

"My mother had to take a number of steps," said Celena. "First, she had to give herself permission to tell her friends, which was difficult for her. Then she eventually allowed me to bring my girlfriend home. There were times she felt good about it, and then a comment or event would come up and we would take a step backward."

Lesbians want to maintain their close ties with their families, particularly their mothers. The mother–daughter bond may have weakened during their years of concealment and now they want to reconnect to their mothers in an authentic way. Most do not consider disclosure an act of defiance, but rather a way of expressing love by being truthful.

Coming Out to Her Father

"I told my father first—I consider myself Daddy's little girl. He was very matter-of-fact in accepting it and asked how we should tell my mother," a 22-year-old woman said. Her father was most concerned about the difficulties that lay ahead for her. He warned her about the hazards of belonging to a persecuted minority. Although mothers' reactions are usually noted in studies, fathers too play a role in lesbians' acceptance of themselves and their ability to lead fully integrated lives.

Those whose fathers have resisted acceptance or have refused to believe their daughters' announcement feign an attitude of indifference. A wall arises between daughter and father that is difficult but not impossible to dismantle. "My father's not accepting of anything," reported a 28-year-old. "I painted him into a corner once and said, 'You don't need to approve of me, you need to tolerate me.' He said, 'I will never tolerate you.'" He outwardly accepts her because her mother does, but his hurtful comment still lingers in her mind.

It has been suggested that it takes two years for parents to recover from learning their daughter is homosexual and to fully accept that reality. Coincidently, the same amount of time is needed to grieve over the death of a loved one.[8] Perhaps some fathers need more time to work through feelings of rejection, for they know they were their daughters' first models of maleness.

Redefining Herself

When a woman defines herself as a lesbian, she must reconstruct her vision of herself, of how she will fit into a heterosexual society. "What was hard was accepting the battle of being a lesbian," a young woman wrote to me. "Picking up the sword, so to speak, and fighting for myself and others. It would have been a lot easier in many ways to blend or assimilate. I feared and I continue to fear others' negative reactions—from the Bible thumpers to the regular homophobes."

Finding a circle of friends who will accept them is important to young lesbians, as with any group of 20- to 30-year-old women. But it may be harder for lesbians to accomplish. One young woman reported that many years before she moved into the town where she now lives, there was a strong community of lesbians. But when the two leaders' partners left them, one for the other, the organization crumbled. "Networking was too threatening after that," she said. Now the closest "gay bars" are one to two hours away, and they are mostly male.

When I asked her who knew she was a lesbian, she replied, "People that are important to me, I told them out right. I have allowed coworkers and casual straight friends to figure it out for themselves." Her closest friends, which include some married couples, are straight, and she and her partner feel very much at ease with them. But she wishes she could connect with some lesbian groups.

Another young woman, age 21, who still struggles with her

sexual identity, told me that she sometimes wonders if it's a passing phase. Even though she has come out to her parents, she has not found a good lesbian relationship. All her partners have been difficult, and "with every failed relationship, I fear I'm not gay." Although she has received support from her family, friends, and coworkers, she is beginning to doubt and is not ready to fully integrate her sexuality into her psyche. "I'm uncomfortable with many lesbian women," she admits. She needs time to sort through her own issues and remains *fluid*, a term used to describe women who may have periods of lesbian attachments.

Some students find themselves in colleges that are considered safer for lesbians and are urged to experiment, try out lesbianism. One young woman told me that her school had many *four-year lesbos*, a term describing peer-pressured relationships. This phenomenon does not necessarily lead a woman to a permanent definition of herself as a lesbian. This fluidity—moving from a lesbian to a heterosexual relationship (and vice versa)—is noted in studies of lesbians but less in the studies of gay men.[9]

When a woman is comfortable with her homosexuality and no longer feels it necessary to continually think of herself in sexual terms only, then she has integrated her sexual identity into her life. "Homosexual identities are most fully realized," wrote sociologist R. R. Troiden, "when self-identity, perceived identity and presented identity coincide; that is, where an accord exists among who people think they are, who they claim they are, and how others view them."[10]

Mothers

Hearing the News

"I'm going through menopause, and my daughter tells me she's a lesbian," moaned one mother. Her daughter's timing could not have been worse as far as she was concerned. Feeling miserable about herself, her daughter's announcement made her feel like a complete failure.

"I had always been very feminine and homophobic in the sense that it always revolted me, the thought of women loving other women," confided another mother of a lesbian. When her daughter told her that she was bisexual, "It was my worst fear come true," she recalled. She kept hoping that her daughter would find a man, but whenever her daughter dated men, she was unhappy. Her daughter, by saying she was bisexual, was paving the way for herself—and her mother—to acknowledge that she was a lesbian.

This mother's initial reaction was shock, despair, self-blame; common reactions to a daughter's coming out. Another mother reported that she took her daughter's news quite calmly and was amazed she didn't react more emotionally. But she conceded: "There was that pit in the stomach that says, 'Oh my God, this is a real situation that we're going to have to deal with.' We didn't know what we were dealing with, what it was going to mean, how hard it was going to be for her and for us and for our family in general."

Most mothers are consumed by an overwhelming heartache and sense of loss. The visions they had for their daughters, their shared lives as wives and mothers, must be altered. Mothers may have been looking forward to the closeness and affection that arise when mothers and daughters become grandmothers and mothers—the shared experiences of women through the ages. Now mothers must reconstruct their understanding of their daughters, of who they truly are, and of what the future may hold for them.

A study that looked at mothers' attitudes following their daughters' disclosures showed that mothers experience a sequence of "confusion, devastation and loss, struggle to come to terms with their daughter's lesbianism, increasing tolerance, and finally an acceptance followed by a residual regret."[11] This sequence may take years as mothers slowly understand that their daughters' decision to come out can improve the mother-daughter relationship by facilitating honest communication.

"Where have we gone wrong?" Sylvia asked as we conversed by phone. This mother was questioning not her own or her family's role in her daughter's lesbianism, but society's. Her daughter had recently come out, and Sylvia was desperately seeking answers. "Our society accepts all kinds of sexual behavior," she moaned. She wondered which came first, society's permissiveness or her daughter's homosexuality. She was sure that the introduction of "alternative lifestyles" encourages children to experiment. They experiment, she claimed, like the feeling, and then think of themselves as gay. Her reaction is not uncommon. Parents initially attempt to blame something, someone, anything for their daughters' homosexuality. Because they cannot pinpoint any certain event or person, most parents eventually stop the blaming game and conclude that their daughters were born lesbian.

A study that interviewed 402 parents of gay and lesbian children asked parents why they thought their children were homosexuals (they could respond in multiple ways). Eighty-seven percent thought their children were "born that way." Ten percent believed it was the way their children were reared. Six percent thought it was the influence of gay friends, and 17 percent didn't know. Interestingly, the parents of daughters, like the woman above, thought their daughters might be more vulnerable to influences of others than did parents of sons.[12]

Isabelle is convinced her daughter was born gay: "I believe her sexuality was determined in utero. There are gay members on both sides of our families." Even though Isabelle rationally accepts the inevitability of her daughter's sexuality, she was heartbroken when her daughter told her. The "residual effect" acknowledged in research lingers for many years.

Mothers are usually taken by surprise by their daughters' announcements, but, with the advantage of hindsight, some can recall personality traits or events that, on reflection, may have given them some warning. The traits mentioned, however, were usually stereotypical characteristics (working actively for women's rights, enjoying the company of women, making anti-male statements) that could be attributed to heterosexual as well as homosexual women.

"When my daughter came out to me," one mother reported, "I can't say I was 100 percent surprised, but 90 percent. She is quite masculine looking, athletic, and interested in women's issues, but I think it's unfair to judge a woman by her masculinity or a man by his femininity because in both cases they are not going to be what you expect." She knew that many lesbian women are very feminine in their demeanor.

The fact that a daughter has lived a dual life, often for many years, adds to a mother's distress and sadness. When she discovers that a roommate has been more than a roommate, she feels deceived. But then she may admit that her daughter was wise not to disclose earlier because she was not ready to hear that news. When Isabelle met her daughter's roommate, she liked her immediately. Like good roommates everywhere, the two shared many interests and quickly became fast friends. A couple of years later, Isabelle's daughter announced that her roommate was also her lover. Isabelle, realizing that her daughter had never been "so happy," accepted her coming out more quickly than she would have if she had not observed them together.

Marian always "loved" her daughter Charlotte's high-school teacher. She had taught her older daughter, too, and always engaged Charlotte's class in exciting debates, inviting a few students over for dinner and evening discussions. When Charlotte started coming home later and later, Marian's husband expressed concern about the relationship, that "something was up" between the two of them. Marian, however, dismissed his apprehensions because she remembered spending wonderful evenings with teachers in her all-girl school. Her other daughter had been tragically killed a short time before, and Marion understood that this daughter needed someone who could share her pain. She was happy that Charlotte had found an empathetic, older friend.

When Marian and her husband went away for a weekend, Charlotte, instead of staying with a friend as planned, flew to her teacher's vacation home. She suddenly became quite ill and was hospitalized. Marian flew home and then to her daughter's bedside. Her daughter, from her sickbed, accused her mother of being responsible for her illness. She loved her teacher, she said, and her mother didn't approve.

"I saw her sitting in that bed, looking like her sister, and I thought, It's happening again. I was losing another child. I couldn't change it with her sister, but maybe I could change it with her. I decided then and there, in that tremendous moment, that this is what she was [a lesbian], and there was nothing I could do about it. I would have done anything for her. Unconditional love is what I have for my children, and that means that, sometimes, you go through hell for it."

The pain of losing one child through death and the fear of losing another through alienation were almost more than Marian could bear. She had no choice but to accept the situation. Although she admired her daughter's teacher, she said, "I could understand the intellectual and mental attraction, but I couldn't understand the physical attraction. It blew my mind."

Marian's previous "love" for the teacher helped her over the next few difficult years. Charlotte went to a college that was accepting of lesbian relationships, and her teacher came for weekends, stayed at the dorm, and spent vacations with her. Charlotte and the teacher remained a couple for many years. Now that they have broken up, Marian misses the many times the three of them had great discussions over dinner. She had truly embraced her daughter's choice.

When Marian looks back on her parenting days, she says, "I brought my children up to stand up for what they believed in. I always was into minority issues myself." When Charlotte went "on the hustings" for lesbian causes, she told her mother, "You taught me how to advocate." But Marian does not feel comfortable advocating for her daughter's gay rights, not yet.

The decision to join their daughters in championing gay rights depends solely on the personalities and instincts of the mothers. Marian did not feel compelled to march or demonstrate. "I'm always glad when the gay parade is on a weekend when I'm out of town," she said. "But I couldn't say no if she asked." Others were involved in their own causes like prison reform or the environment or worked in jobs that didn't allow much free time. Their daughters' gay rights activities remained their own specialty.

An organization called Parents and Friends of Lesbians and Gays (P-FLAG) offers opportunities for parents to meet other parents of lesbians, to receive helpful information, to openly discuss their concerns, and to listen to lesbians and gay men talk about their lives and hopes. Not all mothers are comfortable joining groups to discuss their concerns. They are willing to work with their lesbian daughters without group support. However, many parents develop a network of empathetic friends through P-FLAG, and the organization is open to all parents who want to communicate better with their lesbian daughters.

A study that examined the attitudes of ten mothers of lesbian daughters found that the mothers and daughters struggle with "similar feelings of loss and residual sorrow."[13] They each feel like members of a minority and fear social isolation. Just as their daughters desire to conceal their lesbianism for a time, so do their mothers. Often they each seek counseling. Those mothers in the study who became active in organizations like P-FLAG identified that move as a marker toward acceptance of their daughters' sexuality.

In the study, the mothers who seemed to adapt the easiest (always with some residual sorrow) to their daughters' coming out were college-educated women who worked while their children were growing up and were involved in political and social-justice issues. They also liked their daughters' partners.

The women for whom the disclosure was most painful did not attend college and were not engaged in outside work or social causes. Aside from their close friends and extended family, they had limited life experience. The loss of a traditional daughter wounded them deeply.

The next major step a mother takes in her recognition of her daughter's homosexuality is to share her daughter's coming out with friends and extended members of her family.

Telling Friends

When Elena told her mother she was a lesbian, her mother immediately thought of how her own friends would react to this news. For women like Elena's mother, brought up in a generation that did not tolerate or even recognize lesbians, one of the hardest tasks they face is sharing their daughters' revelations.

"I don't know anyone who has a lesbian daughter," claimed Brenda. She knows young women who talk about their lesbian sisters, but that is all. Yet I had spoken with mothers of lesbians who live in her community—mothers whom she knew. A mother's first impulse is to hope her daughter's attraction to women will go away, just as a daughter hopes when she first suspects she is "different." Even when a daughter wants her mother to share her story (sometimes demands that she does), a mother may hesitate. She is afraid that people won't know how to respond when she says her daughter is a lesbian. Daughters often have the same fear. Before telling someone she is a lesbian, one daughter said she always pauses before she speaks, weighing the risks of being rejected.

"I thought it would not be a problem for me to talk about it," continued Brenda, "but I found I was making my friends uncomfortable, so my hesitancy came from putting them in an uncomfortable position." Brenda still finds herself, not infrequently, in the company of people who make jokes about homosexuals. Their insensitivity awakened her to the complexity of disclosure. She decided she would only tell people when she had enough time for a conversation. She would not, for instance, tell someone who inquired about her daughter if they met on the street or at a large gathering. Brenda wanted her friends to know so they would not make jokes or find out the news from someone else. "I don't care if they don't like us now because we have a homosexual daughter. That's their problem," she said. "The real problem for me is finding the right situation to talk and make them comfortable." Anxious to have her friends continue to value and love her daughter, she wants to explain her daughter's homosexuality the "right way" and not leave it to rumors.

"My friends were absolutely livid that this could happen," said Marian, "but I truly believed that Charlotte was as much in love with her teacher as she was with my daughter." She tried to persuade her friends to think of her daughter and her daughter's lover not as a lesbians, but as they had always thought of them—as bright, attractive, interesting young women.

Telling extended members of the family can trigger a major crisis. Just as a daughter constantly fears being rejected by those she loves, so does her mother. Relatives, both male and female, may exclude a family from festive occasions because they don't want to encounter a lesbian and her partner. A mother is torn because she wants everyone to be happy: her daughter, her daughter's partner, and her extended family. If her daughter disdains traditional women's attire or openly displays her affection for her partner, the situation is exacerbated. Those who feel uncomfortable usually talk with the mother, not the daughter herself. One mother said that her sister keeps asking what her daughter and partner "do" (sexually). She replied, "I don't care what they do. I have respect and love for her because she is my daughter, and that's what counts."

Accepting a Daughter's Partners

Each step on the road to the integration of a daughter's homosexuality into the family entails both heartache and courage. Opening up both heart and home to a daughter's partner, particularly if she appears unconventional, takes time and requires a daughter's, and mother's, patience. Parents who have not allowed a daughter and a boyfriend to share a bedroom in their home until they are married are now faced with a daughter and her girlfriend. Do the parents change their house rules, or are lesbians, because they cannot legally marry, beyond the rules?

Questions such as these arise in families unprepared for the nontraditional behavior of their daughters. Some mothers, fearful of losing their daughters, bend all such rules. Others request that the couple receive the same treatment as their heterosexual sisters or brothers. Even families who are relaxed about heterosexual couples staying together may balk at extending the same hospitality to a lesbian partner.

"It was the biggest hurdle we had to cross," reported one mother. "We never put them in a room with a double bed, so she eventually backed down and stopped requesting it."

Because lesbian couples break up as frequently as heterosexual couples do, parents have to adjust to new women in their daughter's life. That can be especially tough if the coming out partner was a woman they liked and, therefore, helped to soften the blow of their daughter's homosexuality. But a new partner, again and again and again? I heard many times, "She's nice, but not as nice as . . ."

Daughters want their mothers to embrace their partners, to

include them in family events—and family pictures. One daughter mentioned that her partner was deliberately left out of "family only" photos. But I remember excluding my daughters' boyfriends from official family photos, suspecting that they might not be the boyfriends next year. Lesbian daughters who remain sensitive about such issues must be patient. When they have long-term partners, the situation may well change.

Although these issues may be considered "petty" by some, a lesbian daughter may think they are critical indicators of her parents' approval.

Advice from Mothers and Daughters

When I asked mothers what advice they would give to other mothers of lesbians, the answers varied but the clear message was "keep loving your daughter."

"I think, no matter what your religion," responded Lille, "we are going to see more and more homosexuality in the twenty-first century, and the sooner a parent comes to terms with it the happier she will be. Fighting it is fruitless. If that's the sexuality your child has, nothing is going to change her. I want to demystify homosexuality and try to foster acceptance. That's why I'm so open about it."

Daughters also advised their mothers to keep trying, not to give up on communicating. "Communicate even when the process for both gets tough," advised a daughter. "It's not a neat linear progression. Events and milestones prompt resonations, and the issues are revisited through the life cycle."

Both mothers and daughters wanted others to understand that a lesbian daughter can lead a normal life, have a nice home and good job.

"Educate us, be patient, help us to understand where you're

coming from," pleaded one mother. Parents who must reconstruct their vision of their daughter cannot do it overnight, and they ask for time to adjust to this new image.

Daughters who want unequivocal approval for their lifestyle cannot expect to receive it quickly. A mother whose daughter wrote her a scathing letter has adjusted to her daughter's sexuality and welcomes her partner, but still recalls the letter with heartache. A daughter who feels she needs to confront her mother should do it in person. A letter's words can be engraved in a mother's heart and not easily erased. A direct discussion, recalling times of understanding as well as hurt, will resolve the issues more easily.

Marian summed up the feelings of many mothers and daughters. "Life is so precious. I can't imagine life without Charlotte. That's who she is, so there's no question. It's such a joy to be a friend of hers. Don't waste any time not loving your children."

And loving one's daughter includes loving her totally, everything about her, including her sexuality.

10

Searching for
Spiritual Connections

"Whenever I felt low or discouraged," said a 27-year-old, reflecting on her college years, "I would find a place that had a beautiful view of the sunset and just sit and think. That was my church." The memory of that special place still brings peace to this young woman, who currently lives in a crowded metropolitan area. She seeks a similar place of comfort and solace but has not discovered any to replace her college "church." She is not alone in her desire to find a sanctuary for tranquillity and contemplation.

When I began interviewing young women in their twenties and women in midlife, I did not envision writing about their spiritual lives. So many women, however, spoke of their search for something beyond their immediate experience, their longing to find a place of comfort, their need for a spiritual connection, that I decided their voices should be heard.

Many of the women, both mothers and daughters, have been raised in traditional religions, and some still attend their church, synagogue, or temple regularly. However, both those who attend and those who do not attend, traditionalists and nontraditionalists alike, are restless, searching for something more than what they get at a weekly service. Often they are unable to define *more*, describing only a vague notion of something "other."

Neither mothers nor daughters feel obligated to steadfastly follow traditional paths of worship. Freed during the sixties and seventies from traditional constraints on women, they envision other routes to spiritual growth or religious leadership. The previous generation, their grandmothers, found direction and deepened their faith by sitting quietly through a service, saying a rosary, contemplating in an empty church, doing works of charity, or praying to themselves during a busy day. Grandmothers did not have opportunities to explore other avenues of self-renewal or spiritual guidance. Their daughters and granddaughters do.

Mothers

Midlife women, and their daughters, fall through the cracks of the foundations of major religions. Most religious institutions cater to families with children or to older women who help in the volunteer and caretaking duties of the place of worship. Vital women whose children are out of school, who may or may not be employed, and who have many years until they are deemed "elderly" must look elsewhere for their spiritual needs.

They and their daughters sound astonishingly alike as they discuss their dissatisfaction with traditional religions that fail to offer a direction in this stage of their lives. They look for alternatives, sometimes within the framework of their religion but often on the edges.

"All Solutions Are Spiritual"

Myra, a 55-year-old mother, made a voyage "spiritually through the East and ended up in the New Testament." She spent many hours discussing her aspirations with a professor who wrote about spiritual journeys and conducted group discussions. She said that her experiences in that group convinced her that "all problems are psychological, and all solutions are spiritual." When I asked her how she applied that theory in real-life situations, she replied that whenever she had serious communication problems with her daughter, she would force herself to remember that her daughter was an "extension of the infinite." Then Myra could "relax into love" and give her daughter the strength she needed. "What works is not interaction," she said. "What works is inner action." Myra wept as she told of her efforts not to take her daughter's behavior personally. She struggled to reach out to her while working on her own spiritual growth.

As I listened to Myra's story, I realized how her spiritual search had fortified her—in spite of her daughter's rejection and anger. One time, for instance, she had to hop on a plane, find her daughter (then 17), and bring her home, away from peers who were luring her to a lifestyle that Myra knew would be harmful. Myra persevered through her daughter's attempts to run away again and again. Now her daughter, age 22, lives in a nearby town, works, and goes to school part-time. She thanks her mother for not losing faith in her.

Myra does not go to church but uses the Bible as a teaching tool and applies its lessons to her own life. She epitomizes the shift that is happening as women turn from therapy to self-directed spirituality as a guide to mental health. Although she and her daughter also sought psychological help, Myra realized that the complete resolution of their relationship lay elsewhere. For Myra, developing her inner life helped her overcome what seemed to be insurmountable obstacles.

Economics is also hastening the reliance on spiritual explorations as an alternative to psychological or medical solutions to problems. With insurance companies placing limits on mental-health visits and the emergence of books, television shows, Web sites, and organizations that link mental and physical health with the spiritual, many people, like Myra, are turning to spiritual resolutions of their conflicts. Mental- and medical-health professionals are shifting away from exploring past transgressions to focusing on present behavior. They offer guidelines, and many sanction alternative therapies, including prayer and meditation. Psychologists report using meditation as a way for patients to find "their inner sense of identity," while some practitioners think meditation "lies at the heart of efforts to treat addiction."[1] This shift is aided by the recent media attention on the phenomenon of psychic healings and a heightened interest in the practice of Eastern forms of meditation, yoga, and herbal cures.

Women in midlife are drawn to alternative ways of expressing their inner life, not because of faddish impulses but because they are seeking balance in their lives. Their experience within families has given them insight, maturity, strength, and resilience, which lead to wisdom and balance, but they need more. Can mainstream religions that have been caught up in their own struggle to maintain their institutional structures reach out to a congregation of educated, mature women? From my conversations with women, the answer for the most part is no. Not many religious institutions offer them a home for spiritual growth. They find opportunities elsewhere.

The Problem

The spiritual guidebooks that appear annually on best-seller lists confirm the continued interest with the search for the spiritual. Why haven't mainstream religions joined their people in this quest? Are they threatened when women seek out small groups and discuss their personal faith without the presence of clergy? Are they intimidated by women who want to live by a message of the spirit rather than the dogma of a church?

Most women who engage in a spiritual journey (not a fundamentalist revival) want to join a congregation that does not single out any person or group for discrimination. Women who have borne children, who have lived through rejection by spouse or children, who have agonized over a daughter or son's unhealthy path, who have nursed sick family members or watched a beloved parent die do not need to be preached at. They know that loving acceptance of all people with their failings—and, yes, their sins—reflects a true nobility of spirit. They are not looking for rules and regulations but for open arms. They, in their nurturing roles, have offered open arms to relatives and friends in need and cannot comprehend why religious institutions argue over supposed human failings rather than embracing humanity.

"At some point organized religion did not work for me" was a theme I heard often. These women have rejected traditional religion not because of some whim, but because their experiences with the institution were negative or they did not feel any uplifting or practical application from attending services. Many women, however, still speak of the beauty of the ritual and miss the familiar hymns of their childhood.

This disaffection with religious institutions often arose while their children were still at home and, therefore, influenced how they raised their children. While many mothers continued to worship with a congregation to provide a good example to their children, they now say they raised their children to be "good people." They do not categorize "good people" into religious sects. They brought their children up to be inclusive, not divisive.

Women in midlife, who no longer feel obligated to attend a service on a regular basis, have the freedom to explore other options. "What I think is open to women at this point is the opportunity to really begin to explore the other parts of ourselves," confirmed a woman who has rejected her religion. Many see a direct link between physical health, mental attitude, meditation, and prayer and believe they can make those connections without the intercession of clergy.

Mysticism in the Jewish or Christian traditions, Buddhist meditation, and yoga practice attract these women as well as their daughters. Women whose children are grown want to achieve a balance in their physical, mental, and spiritual lives. They usually have more time then their daughters to actually investigate their interests. One woman told of her determination to take time off from work to travel to Tibet because she is fascinated with the idea of reincarnation. Having experienced psychic encounters, which she never revealed because she thought her family would think she was crazy, she now feels the freedom to pursue them.

"I want to grow spiritually," said another woman, who thought women had lost their connection with the universe. She feared that if she were alive in the Middle Ages, she might have been burned at the stake as a witch because of her desire to experience the mysterious.

These women are not hippies (who still dream of days in Haight-Ashbury). Many hold jobs, have raised families, and on balance seem to be happy and in control of their lives. But they want something more.

Not all women indict traditional religions for not fulfilling their needs. The presence of women clergy has altered some entrenched attitudes toward women, and, because of their influence, more attention is being paid to personal ways of reaching God or communicating religious values. Some congregations are taking the lead. "I get confirmation from my church because I think of myself as a humanitarian," said one woman. Because her church takes "brave and bold" stands on social issues, including the hiring of women ministers, she willingly participates in its leadership. She likes the fact that her church supports active community outreach in areas of social concern *and* offers ongoing opportunities for her to explore her inner life. If more churches followed that example, midlife women might be knocking on their doors.

Kathleen Norris, in her best-selling books about her own spiritual journey, writes of rediscovering not only her spiritual roots in her grandparents' Protestant community but also her poetic nature in a community of cloistered Catholic monks. She had lived for many years in a bustling urban center and had lost the capacity to focus on her spiritual life. The move to her family's homestead in the Great Plains of South Dakota awakened her soul.[2]

Most women are not able, as Kathleen Norris was, to travel to new areas. They yearn to awaken their inner vistas and reclaim their souls while remaining at home. Midlife offers a chance for deeper spiritual connections no matter where one is located.

The Appeal of the Alternative

Eva, a 54-year-old therapist, recalled her early exposure to religion. "I can remember when I was 14 and being sworn in as a new member of a church. I was asked to write a letter to myself which I would receive in the mail a year later about this experience. I don't think I used the word *bullshit*, but that's how I felt. That was much too small for what it's all about. I've never liked people to place labels on others. Each person is an individual in her or his own right and is part of whatever the larger evolving energy is."

Eva now can articulate what was bothering her at age 14, that she did not want to be labeled as belonging to one congregation. In the last five years she has moved to a "more spiritual plane" both personally and with clients. She is drawn to an Eastern type of philosophy, which she described as "one day at a time, live in the moment. Worries are in the past and in the future, so you might as well just stay in today and do the best you can."

Part of her therapeutic agenda is to nurture in her clients that philosophy—the capacity to live in the present. She also wants to enlarge their perceptions so they will not be judgmental of other people's religions or lifestyles. Her personal faith grows deeper as she herself learns to accept others, but she still has not found a church that matches her philosophy.

In many towns across the country, yoga classes, prayer groups, unauthorized rituals are supplementing or replacing weekly religious services. "I'm hungry for an experience of Christ in my life," said a 55-year-old who seldom goes to church. "I'm spending a lot of time on Bible study in an ecumenical group, and I seem to be trying to grow in that area more than anything else. The rest of my life seems to be a lot of minutiae."

In these smaller groups, women talk freely of their fears, joys, worries, and accomplishments without being made to feel insignificant, boring, or irrelevant.

The Expected Role—Focus on the Other

Is it true that women only find happiness when they sacrifice themselves for others? This traditional view—proclaimed by many religions—that a woman finds fulfillment only when she puts her own needs on hold has been discarded by most women. As women look back on turning points in their lives, many recall that when they did not speak up about a situation, a relationship shifted, but not for the better. They thought they were helping the family by withholding their own feelings. But the lack of open dialogue between spouses or between mother and child can come to a head in later years when a woman releases her flow of words and takes the family by surprise. By then her family is not accustomed to listening to her, does not take her seriously, or is hurt by her outburst.

As women become attuned to expressing themselves and realize that their opinions have merit, they begin to think about their own needs. But a dramatic shift from never thinking about one's self to full concentration on self can disturb the balance. The finding of oneself, which is part of a spiritual exploration, takes years. A woman who has not allowed her true self to emerge must move slowly, but resolutely, to find a comfortable expression of self.

"Finding yourself is such a slow process," said a mother and physician, age 56. "It probably takes at least fifty years. There is nothing rigid about the self. The self is learning and changing, so what you are yesterday you are probably not today, and what you thought yesterday may not come back today, so you have to be flexible."

Most women would agree with her description of self. A woman learns and changes from exposure to other people, to other ways of thinking, to stages in life.

"I do believe," she went on to say, "that the self cannot constantly come first." When I asked her what, then, is the highest value she could pass on to her daughters, she replied, "Integrity to themselves and service to others."

Integrity and service go hand in hand. "From a spiritual perspective, service is a good working definition of spirituality in action," writes Joan Borysenko, former director of the Mind/Body Clinic at Harvard Medical School. She notes that all major religions are firmly rooted in service.[3]

The concept of being true to oneself while remaining true to those with whom we live, work, and serve touches the core value of inner life. Women who follow that course of true integrity will not end up frustrated, angry that they have sacrificed for others without developing their own mind, spirit, and body. They will have found a balance of service and self-development that will carry them through all stages of their lives.

The spiritual restlessness expressed by midlife women is reflected at another level by young women in their twenties. Daughters often respond to unspoken messages ("vibes") from their mothers, and their attitudes toward religion seem to be spun from their mothers' inner thoughts.

Daughters

Young single women do not ponder religious faith in terms of what they will teach to their children, as their older married sisters might. They think instead of the present; the help, comfort, or companionship a religion does or does not bring to them as they progress through their difficult first decade out of school. Because women make personal decisions during their twenties that will affect them for years, they look for support and advice. Sometimes it's welcome from family and friends. Often they want to talk with a group of peers (beyond their immediate circle) who share their values. Some women are lucky to find small communities of young adults who provide that support, sometimes within their own religious tradition.

Renewal in Traditional Religions

Kitty graduated from college three years ago, has a good job, a steady boyfriend, and a strong bond with her mother. Her mother introduced her to some "wonderful, beautiful religious stuff," and they have gone together on weekend retreats to discuss their faith. Kitty learned the value of faith from her mother's recent personal experiences. She has seen her mother, who has undergone some very difficult personal and financial times during the last few years, strengthened by faith. She attributes her mother's newly found coping skills to a renewal of faith through a Charismatic group.

Kitty witnessed healings through a friend of her mother and, after a spiritual awakening herself during a retreat, joined a Charismatic young-adult group. Kitty described herself in traditional terms as a Catholic. Yet she admitted that most of her friends are skeptical of church bureaucracy and won't be part of it. She doesn't dispute their problems with the church (especially birth control, abortion, and sexist attitudes) and agrees with many of their points. She looks at the church as a place to receive the sacraments. But her heart is with her Charismatic friends, who meet regularly outside the confines of a Sunday service. Kitty has found a growing community of people whom she can trust. She values the fun of their meetings, the "lightheartedness" of the group, and their commitment to follow the teachings of Jesus.

Religious renewal is a rising phenomenon among young people. The Charismatic movement, or the Pentecostal movement as it is called in Protestant sects, touches deep emotions and satisfies many young women's need to belong to a community, to be respected, to have an unfailing place to turn to depend on something other than human vagaries, to sing in worship. Dogmas are replaced with giving praise to God, and emphasis is placed on the gifts (charisms) of God.

Within Jewish communities, many also are reexamining their spiritual roots, meeting in homes in groups called Chavurah (Hebrew for community). Also wanting to avoid bureaucracy and get to the "heart of the matter," they study and learn and celebrate together. Some Jewish centers are sponsoring "Discovery" seminars targeted at young adults. By using a "code" method of interpreting the scriptures, the seminars present a skeptical generation with an intellectual basis for belief in God.[4]

Some young women find renewal through tragedy. "I don't go to church very often," said Nicki. "I think you have to find it within, but I have had a definite revelation about spirituality." Nicki's best friend from college died a year after graduation. Her friend had been active in a small religious Christian community. After his death, his parents asked Nicki to join them in meditations with a spiritual guide who was part of their son's community. The meditations opened up Nicki's eyes to the possibility of relating to her "inner spirit" in a wholly different way.

Her friend's family held a party at his grave, complete with music and food, and it was "the most empowering experience I've had," Nicki said. The weekend renewed her self-confidence, which had plummeted since graduating from college, and reassured her that she could "make it." She met later with the spiritual guide, who advised her to have her "chart" read because he felt such strength from her. Nicki was drawn to this exercise but, because of the expense, has delayed. Nicki identifies herself in traditional terms as a Protestant Christian. She calls her experience a "renewal" because it brought her back to her early religious feelings, but not to the traditional expression of those feelings. She connects to this small community within the larger Christian framework.

Renewal may be personal or communal, but its key elements are an emotional uplifting and a return to some practices of the early years of religious communities. These practices may range from speaking in tongues, to bearing witness to being saved, to making a commitment to a savior, to rededicating oneself to the church or synagogue of childhood.

Many mainstream religions recognize this desire for renewal among the young and are striving to meet it. The Center for Ministry Development, after interviewing young adults from across the country and, in addition, surveying one thousand young adults, reported the top ten religious needs of young people ages 18 to 32 were: membership in a community; dynamic liturgies; religious education; guidance and direction in life; acceptance and support; opportunities for service and leadership; social activities; a community that has common values; personal inspiration; rejuvenation.[5]

This survey reflects the needs I heard young women express. But how quickly can religious institutions meet the yearnings of young adults who may have turned away from their messages?

Looking Beyond the Institution

"I don't believe in the institution of the church," said one young woman. Like Nicki, she is confused about what she wants or can believe. She mentioned, for instance, that a friend's death disturbed her greatly, and the only place she could find solace was in an empty church. In spite of finding that refuge in time of pain, she doesn't believe a church can fulfill her spiritual needs. She credits her parents with giving her a deep sense of service, which she considers more important than going to church. Her parents gave up practicing their religion when she was in high school. Although they did not share a religion with their daughter during her adolescent years, they shared the message of service which is espoused by all world religions. She finds her areas of service outside, not inside, the church. She accepts all religions but does not want to be coerced into joining one.

The openness that this young woman proclaims dismays many clergy as they see the young members of their congregations slip away through marriage in another faith or indifference to any faith. Most young women don't consider a boyfriend's religion an obstacle to a relationship or to marriage. These women represent the ultimate democratization of American life. All religions are equal in their minds. That does not mean they do not appreciate their own tradition, but it does mean that they do not demean others. Conscious of both Christmas and Hanukkah commemorations at their winter assemblies, they learned that exposure to other religions could enrich their lives.

Gail, who identifies herself as a born-again Christian, has been active in a group of young Christians since her high-school days. But at times she dislikes the intolerance she finds. "I get frustrated with Christians who think it has to be one way," she said. "It just makes me crazy. I think they don't understand anything. I really have a hard time with them." She joined a student Christian group during her freshman year in college but concluded its focus was too narrow. The members even frowned upon going to parties, not wanting students to associate with noncommitted people. She also became frustrated with the intolerance she found in some study groups on campus: "I was involved in a couple of Bible studies, but they were not very accepting of gays and lesbians, and I just wonder how anyone will ever understand what you're talking about if you're intolerant. It's such a contradiction to say I'm a Christian and I love everyone, but I don't like you."

A majority of American young people have been raised in homes that espouse a religion. A survey of 18 to 70 year olds taken by the National Opinion Research Center of the University of Chicago reported that in the age category of 18 to 29, 52 percent say they were raised Protestant, 35 percent Catholic, 2 percent Jewish, and 3 percent "other." Eight percent were not raised in any religion. The 8 percent represents the highest percentage in any age group that has been raised without any religious affiliation—a concern for the future of organized religion.[6]

Exposure to their parents' religion when they were children does not mean that young women are following in their parents' religious footsteps. Many are framing their own attitudes.

"I had to go to church every Sunday until my junior year in high school," Robin, age 24, said as she told of how she would try to "con" her way out of church every week. Her mother recently died, and she hoped she would have a "revelation" after her mother's death, but she did not. Although she thinks fondly back on the rituals of her childhood faith, she doesn't feel the need to reenter the church. She wants something "other."

"There was no choice in my home," said Anita, who had to go to church three times a week during her first 18 years. "The first time I had my freedom, I rejected everything." In college, Anita and her friends would stay up late into the night discussing religion, spirituality, the moral issues they were facing. She came to the conclusion that she didn't believe in any institutional religion. She thinks, however, that there is a God and that it's important for people to have a sense of spirituality, a "sense of your place in the greater world, not in the physical world, but in this big realm of existence."

Anita envies her parents, who have a secure faith and believe that if they follow the prescribed way, they will go to heaven. She has not found a religion that can give her that security.

The majority of young people, 53 percent, still firmly believe in God. That percentage is the lowest among all age groups. Other 18- to 29-year-olds believe in varying degrees. Twenty-one percent believe but have doubts; 4 percent believe sometimes; 8 percent believe in a higher power; 6 percent don't know if there is a God and have no way to find out, and 4 percent don't believe in God at all.[7]

The decrease in the number of young people asserting a firm faith in God or acknowledging membership in a church worries institutions that look to serve the young and that depend on them to carry on their message. The yearning for a connection to something other than their daily existence propels many young women to seek out a religion. But time and time again young women are disappointed with what they find within the four walls of the place of worship.

Where Are the Churches?

Most congregations don't know how to approach young women to attract them to the fold. Some individual congregations, often in the midst of urban gentrified areas, have established service and social programs that attract young people. However, traditional congregations, those that focus on family and children and whose rows are filled with the elderly, pass right over a generation of women who are seeking spiritual guidance. Some young women venture out and sample the Sunday (or Saturday) services.

Two women raised in traditional religions have been con-
ducting a "door-to-door" search for "meaningful" services on
Sunday mornings. Every week they attend a different church in
their West Coast city. They are discouraged, however, because
they have not found the right "comfort zone." As one of them
put it, "It's hard to find something that is not too jazzy and has a
little bit of formal stuff and where we can sing and enjoy a community." After a year of visiting churches, they haven't found a
congregation that suits them, but they are not giving up.

The congregations that attract young people can be repli-
cated, but creating a vital, young community takes an enormous
amount of energy and committed volunteers. One young
woman who wanted to return to church because she was getting
married (finding a place to hold the marriage ceremony is often a
motivating force) finally found a church she could fit into. "It's
fresh, younger," she said. "Their [clergy] minds are open. They
don't care if you were married before. They don't care if you
have other things happening in your life. They just say come,
come and be with us and help us. They have a great volunteer
program. It's really like family." She now is bringing members of
her own family to the church.

Congregations can take their cues from the experience of this
young woman and extend the voice of welcome and acceptance.
The message of love and tolerance, which was the message of the
founders of most religions, has been lost with the rise of large
institutions and hierarchies. If religious communities would listen
to the voices of young women, they would hear the clear message of spiritual need.

Values Count

When Johanna, a 29-year-old, commented that she thought
something was wrong with her because she was not "feeling

spiritual," her friends pointed out that her choice of a service career reflected her values—and her early religious training. She objected to their suggestions. "I think my values have something to do with me, not with my religion," she said. "It's more to do with who I am and what's important to me. I guess I just haven't reached the point where I connect spirituality at all with my life."

Johanna has been in and out of therapy because of her struggle with an eating disorder and has thought a lot about herself and her goals. Although she now feels in control of her eating, she is aware that maintaining a heathy mental balance is not easy. But she does not feel the need to seek spiritual counsel to help maintain that balance. When she and her friends were discussing spirituality, she commented that her grandmother "would turn over in her grave" if she knew that Johanna had not been to church since she was young. She depends only on herself. She was surprised to hear her friends discuss their longing for a community where they could worship or celebrate, and she seemed drawn to consider whether she would benefit from such a community herself. She had not known they felt such a need and seemed amazed that they did not consider this need a weakness, a flaw.

Johanna is right that her values determine who she is and how she acts. By the time women reach their midtwenties, they have developed their basic attitudes toward others. Her respect for all people, which was shown by her years working with cooperatives that distributed food to the poor, identifies her as a person with high spiritual values, regardless of her present religious connections.

Young women like Johanna, however, who suffer from an addiction, in her case an eating disorder, would be well advised not to depend on themselves alone and to look into programs similar to Alcoholics Anonymous (AA). One of the twelve steps of AA is the acknowledgment of a dependence on a higher being. Fighting an obsession with something that is as omnipresent as food takes an enormous willpower and a reliance on inner strength. A belief in something other than her own ability can help a young woman calm her inner spirit. But the connection must be authentic and one that satisfies her deepest spiritual needs.

Religion used to offer that connection and still does in some communities. Many mainstream religions, however, have lost a vital segment of their congregations by not reaching out to young women in the years between college and marriage. In reality, the 18- to 29-year-olds are the "lost generation" for mainstream religious institutions.

Finding Alternatives

"For a lot of younger people, orthodoxy does not necessarily touch us," said a 27-year-old as she talked about not needing to attend church in order to be a good person. Instead she wants time to be by herself, with her own thoughts, and communicate with God in her own way.

"I have a strong presence of God in my life," said another 27-year-old. "I don't force it on other people and don't talk about it, but I go for long walks and I think a lot about life and where I'm going."

These two women have found that being alone and meditating enriches them. Because of this attention to meditation, Eastern religions are appealing to young women, not in a traditional sense of believing in the writings or sacred books, but in the outward manifestations of those religions.

The practice of yoga flourishes in many areas of the country. Emphasizing the connectedness of body and spirit, yoga attracts young women, who find that holding a yoga pose supplies a physical challenge and benefits mental health. I heard the sentence "Yoga is great" from many young women. They view the practice as a fresh approach to their daily time out for themselves. Because yoga uses a holistic approach, they believe they are strengthening their bodies and spirits at the same time.

One young woman who was raised in a Western religion took yoga to relieve her stress while she was in law school. Yoga now is her way of meditating. "I really started escaping through yoga meditations," she said. "It allows you to get in touch with your inner spirit. It sounds really crazy, but I definitely believe that there's a spiritual world and spirituality is very important, whatever form it may take."

Another woman who was raised by a "pretty positively Jewish" family now considers herself completely "secular" but will always follow her family's traditional holidays. She also has found time to reflect and "maintain sanity" through the practice of yoga and meditation.

The appeal of these alternative ways reaches women from many backgrounds.

Direct Contact

Although going to a religious service may not be a high priority with young unmarried women, many are aware of the presence of God. "A day doesn't go by when I don't talk to God," one young woman commented. "I feel guilty that I don't go to service, but I feel in some ways I'm more religious than someone who goes every week."

Talking to God is more common than I would have thought. Even for small, trivial items, some young women told me they talked to God. One prayed for a table and found one on a street and laughed as she said she then put in "an order" for an armchair. Acknowledging that her conversations with God are usually more serious, she has developed a natural pattern of talking with God, a direct intercession (called prayer by the clergy).

God is not dead in the lives of young women. Their religious practices may be put on hold, they may harbor doubts as to the existence of God, but their belief in something outside the ordinary is solid.

A Value-Oriented Life

What about women who do not feel the same need for spiritual exploration expressed by the younger and older women in this chapter? They can find a basis for a value-oriented life by listening to their inner guide, their voice of conscience and compassion, and by respecting the voices of others. A belief or trust in God or a spiritual power does not necessarily create a moral person. As once was said, "If you think going to church makes you a Christian, you probably think sitting in a garage makes you a car."

Living a life of integrity, commitment, and service honors the inner spirit of morality that is passed on through generations of women.

Mothers and Daughters: A Common Quest

Mothers and daughters may be surprised to read that their spiritual desires are similar. Mothers sometimes just ignore their negative reactions to religious services and tune out. They often don't voice their feelings to their daughters because they have raised their daughters in a specific religion and want them to maintain a spiritual base.

Daughters, for their part, are not inclined to criticize their mother's religious habits. Daughters are on their own, busy with their own lives, and generally don't talk about spirituality with their mothers. They perhaps think their mothers' faith is secure and nonquestioning. But, deep down, they both desire the same thing—a spiritual connection that brings inner peace, energy, and a sense of completeness—a common quest.

11

The Wedding

Getting Married?
Benefits of Marriage
Postponing Marriage
Making the Decision
Mother and/or Daughter Plan the Event
The Bride and Groom Prepare for a Lifetime
"All You Get Is One Person"
Advice from a Bride and Groom
Mother's Advice
Voices of Young Men
After the Wedding

Getting Married?

In the last half of her twenties and into her early thirties, a young woman is caught up in wedding mania. She finds herself using precious vacation days to fly around the country to friends' weddings. She searches for wedding gifts, and if she serves as a bridesmaid, she will purchase a dress that she may never wear again. It's hard for a young woman to miss the significance of these events for herself. Her days are numbered; her friends are marrying; shouldn't she be thinking about pairing up?

Once she permits her imagination to visualize herself in that role, thoughts about her own wedding emerge. Perhaps she hasn't pictured herself as a bride since she was a child. She has had too many things to see, places to go, a career to start. But as she approaches or passes 30, her dream resurfaces.

Her mother, on the other hand, has never forgotten and has been subtly (and not so subtly) reminding her that time is drawing short, that she really is old enough to get married. As often as she has told her mother to back off and lower her "mother of the bride" expectations, her mother has never given up hope that her daughter will find an exceptional partner. Her mother prays that someday her daughter will be swept away or marry the man she's been with for years.

Many factors contribute to a daughter's decision to marry. No longer is being in love her only criterion. She may have been in love numerous times before she meets the right person to marry. Now other factors will be weighed: Does he support her emotionally? Does he agree with her career ambitions, and does she agree with his? Do they both want children? Are their lifestyles and goals compatible? Are they both "ready" to make this lifelong commitment?

Benefits of Marriage

Most mothers have been preaching the benefits of marriage to their daughters since childhood. Even if a mother has despaired over her own marriage, she wants her daughter to marry. She hopes that her daughter will not repeat her, and her husband's, mistakes. She knows and misses the intimacy, camaraderie, and security that a good marriage offers. A mother wants her daughter to experience the security of a spouse who loves her steadily through good times and bad times, the fun of a spouse who supports her crazy ideas and serious opinions, the support of a spouse who shares her interests and dreams, the comfort of a spouse who embraces her, and the passion of a spouse who loves her.

Research backs up mothers' tributes to marriage. Studies consistently show that married women report they are happier than single women, even young women. A recent study, for example, found that young women and men who get and stay married (the interviewees had been married up to seven years) report higher levels of well-being than those who remain single.[1]

But, as mothers have discovered, their daughters are not

rushing to join this state of well-being. "Marriage is like exercise," one researcher observed. "You have to give people the information and some are going to say, 'I know this is good for me and I am going to push myself and I am going to have a healthier and more satisfying life."[2] But just as advice about exercise is ignored and excuses are made, some women are not ready or willing to take their mothers' advice and commit themselves to a lifelong love affair.

Postponing Marriage

Women marry later because they want to develop themselves first. They have been told since their early years that professionally they can do anything and have anything they work for—if they work hard. Now, in their late twenties, those goals are in sight— or almost. Yet it is easy to keep putting off the idea of marriage because there is always something else to be accomplished.

A 30-year-old woman who was changing careers and entering graduate school explained why she had postponed marriage: "How can two people who have no clue get married? I want to be established before I go into marriage. You know how men want to be established and take care of the woman. Well, I want to be able to take care of myself. Otherwise I'm too susceptible to just going off and following someone around the world." She later said that her goal was to be married by the time she reached 35—her personal deadline. She had turned down a marriage proposal (presented with an engagement ring, so the young man had obviously anticipated a yes) when she was 25 and recently heard that her former boyfriend was getting married. She wept when she heard the news because deep in her heart she still thought of him as a possibility. But her original love for him had not deterred her from deciding to turn him down in order to make a career choice and move to another country. Also, scarred by the memories of her parents' divorce, she wanted to establish her own career and find security on her own first.

Many young women expressed similar sentiments. They are determined to spend some time discovering themselves before committing to marriage. "I came up through school to concentrate on myself, so that's what I'm doing right now," said a 24-year-old recent graduate. "I'm finding what it is that will make me happy because if I'm not happy, no one I'm with will be happy."

At times it was dismaying to hear these women's desire to know themselves so thoroughly so young. Knowing oneself is a lifelong search, and women find themselves (and their abilities) through relationships with others. To concentrate too much on self is to risk losing vital connections to others who will help in the search for meaning. As with so much of life, the key is in the balancing. The fear these women have of losing themselves or their identity in marriage permeates many of their thoughts. Marriage is postponed or relationships are severed until they achieve a sense of individuality.

"We have the ability to be independent," said a 27-year-old who had just left her boyfriend who ran a family business in a small rural town. "It was never a choice before. You were put into a situation where your man was your support. That's who provided for you, and today we have a choice to provide for ourselves. That's an empowerment that you have to embrace, or else you're not taking advantage of what's out there. You don't have to become a brain surgeon or a CEO, but it will make it easier in the long run if you become a little independent and worldly."

She did not think she would find happiness or independence in her boyfriend's rural community. Now, having moved to a West Coast city, she wonders if she will ever find someone as wonderful as her former boyfriend. Still she is confident that her decision to leave him was the right one. She cared about her own way of life and job possibilities and did not think he or his community would support her.

These young women took the risk of losing a potential marriage partner, one whom they genuinely seemed to love, in order to establish themselves. This is a clear difference from their mothers, who put husband, children, and career in that order. Their daughters have moved career to the top position.

Many men today agree that women should be accomplished before marriage—and after—a seismic shift in attitude from previous generations. The National Survey of Families and Households found that single men were willing to marry a woman who made more money and had more education than they did. They were less willing to marry a woman who was unlikely to hold a steady job.[3] If that survey had been given when their mothers were young, men would not have shown the same expectations. In most cases the men had more education than women and did not expect their wives to keep working after getting married or having children.

Another reason women delay marriage until their late twenties or early thirties is that they no longer feel the necessity to explain their single status, as their mothers did. A recent survey reported that during the nineties, 10 percent of men and women under the age of 30 describe themselves as "not too happy." In 1970, 14 percent said they were "not too happy." The researchers noted that the biggest increase in happiness came from unmarried young people, and suggested that "young men and women have benefited from society's recently increased tolerance of those living outside marriage."[4] The societal acceptance of a single woman living alone, with friends, or cohabitating with a man has removed the pressure on her to marry.

The obvious reason why some women delay marriage until they're older is because they have not met the right man. "The idea of spending my life with someone is really foreign," confessed Sonya, age 25. "Trying to comprehend that is difficult, especially with the relationships I've had. I can't imagine being with a person even a month." Sonya has not met the right man.

Making the Decision

Let's say a woman is around 30 and in love with the partner she has been searching for. What is she waiting for? The answer may very well be "nothing," so she decides to get married (and so does he). For some women, pregnancy also prioritizes the decision to marry—urgency becomes a factor. Within a short period, four young women I know married when they became pregnant. They loved their boyfriends, in two cases were living together and planning marriage in the future. The pregnancy hastened their decision. In a way, the situations reminded me of the fifties, when abortion was not legal and many a pregnant bride walked down the aisle. Motherhood still remains a powerful motivation for marriage. "I won't get married until I want a baby," said one 30-year-old. Her boyfriend agrees with her.

The vast majority of women are not pregnant, and the time does come when the right man appears, their "life goals" are similar, she feels ready, and a wedding is planned. They may meet at an indoor rock-climbing wall, a shared summer home, or a charity event (like the couple who met building houses for Habitat for Humanity), at school or work—even in a subway car or on the Internet. Two women met their future husbands through a chat room, moved on to E-mail, discovered they had mutual friends even though they lived in different cities (one even knew the other's relatives), arranged to meet, and became engaged a few years later. When women do meet the right man, an idea that seemed "foreign" is now very appealing.

Mother and/or Daughter
Plan the Event

Even if a mother is not overly excited about her daughter's choice of mate, she inevitably moves into high gear when the engagement is announced. As wedding plans are made, a new dimension is added to the mother-daughter relationship. They become the strategists—plotting, planning, and executing the wedding. *The Wedding* is discussed in minute detail and becomes a focus of their lives.

But a mother soon discovers that the event will not happen exactly as she may have envisioned. A young woman who has lived and worked independently is unlikely to hand her wedding plans over to her mother. She, the bride, wants a major say in her marriage arrangements (if not total control), and a mother should adapt to her wishes.

Although the occasional mother may have had an outdoor wedding in bare feet, chances are most mothers followed family traditions. They allowed their mothers to run the wedding and take credit for the event. Pampered by family and relatives, they were proudly presented by their fathers (who paid all the bills) as virginal brides.

But now, a woman who has participated in (or run) corporate meetings, helped plan policy, worked in public services, or ventured to the far reaches of the earth (and may have lived with the man she will marry) wants a say in her wedding. With half the women marrying for the first time over the age 24.5 years, traditional weddings are being replaced by ceremonies that are more personal or more dramatic. Sometimes the aim is just to be different. The brides themselves may have participated in many weddings (one woman had been in thirteen), and mothers must adjust to their daughters' desires and, yes, expertise.

Although planning for a wedding should, in theory, draw

daughters and mothers closer together, it often turns out quite differently—especially if a mother wants control or is not used to planning large parties. Organizing the myriad details of a wedding requires experience. Not many mothers have entertained one hundred or more (sometimes many more) guests, and just the thought can be overwhelming. Wedding experts are available. However, finding one who will understand the wishes of both generations may be tough. Advice abounds in books and magazines. One young man claims his fiancée ordered a five-year subscription to a bride's magazine the day after he proposed. Cyberspace entered the wedding business early on. Over 202,000 wedding-related Web sites are offered on the Internet, enough to keep a mother and daughter occupied for a full year of preparation.[5]

One young woman suggested that the title of this chapter should be "Mother's Last Stand." Indeed, some mothers think that they will be judged by the wedding and want to bestow all their energy into this departing gesture. They also want to display their creation: an outstanding young woman. Mothers say that friends who have been through the wedding drill are the most helpful—and the most sympathetic. They offer the kind of advice that experts cannot, and they know the importance of keeping a daughter's wishes in the forefront. They often regret the petty arguments they had with their daughters. But some mothers may not be sensitive enough to pick up on their daughters' anger with the plans they are advocating. Daughters become quite adept at concealing their anguish. They sense a mother's nervousness and do not want to disrupt their relationship before the wedding day.

One mother, having read about the pitfalls of planning a wedding and anxious not to alienate her engaged daughter, promised her daughter that the wedding would not disrupt their good relationship. "I told her that nothing (the dress, the guests, the money) was as important as our friendship, and she agreed."

Looking back on her daughter's wedding, she is grateful that they only had three months to plan the festivities. Their options were few, and decisions had to be made quickly—no time for second thoughts or needless worry. At one point she had to remind her daughter that this was a wedding, not a coronation. But, true to their promise, they remained friends.

The cost of the wedding can present many problems. When asked to list the top three expenses they face in midlife, parents named a wedding right along with home improvements and college education.[6] Now when the bride and groom both have been working for a while, they often expect to pay their share of the wedding. And wise parents of the groom can pick up some of the expenses—like the liquor bill, which often adds a substantial figure to the overall expense.

Franny wanted an elegant wedding, but her parents did not. They could not afford an elaborate setting and did not feel comfortable with the high level of sophistication that their daughter wanted. Franny, therefore, along with her fiancé, planned the wedding, paid the bills, and then presented her parents with a bill that her parents could afford. In the end her parents were pleased (although it was not their type of wedding). Everyone was happy. The bride and groom, who had been working in good jobs, had the wedding they wanted, and her parents contributed as much financial support as they were able.

Other mother–daughter pairs discuss the particulars of a wedding until each one is sick of the subject, and laugh at the absurdity of spending sometimes up to a year planning a wedding. Some daughters don't want anything to do with the details and let their mothers rule. But most find some sort of middle ground so each will be happy.

Christie and her mother had never disagreed, at least outwardly, about anything until her wedding. During the seven months between the engagement and the wedding, their phone calls increased in number but decreased in minutes. They were in a struggle for control. Who would decide what? Christie, who had worked for eight years organizing large events, possessed all the expertise needed to plan a wedding. However, her mother wanted Christie, her only daughter, to have the most traditional wedding possible. According to Christie, they disagreed on most things but usually ended up doing what her mother demanded. They even argued about when to open the wedding presents. Who won? It's hard to say. Christie recalls that her relationship with her mother changed when she realized that her mother's big issue was control. She then realized how much of her life had been devoted to acquiescing to her mother's wishes. Since the wedding they have not discussed those difficult months, and their relationship outwardly appears to be the same. But Christie discovered something about herself and her mother that, at some point, they need to discuss.

Control was not an issue with Cindy and her mother. "My mother was cool about everything," Cindy said. But Cindy and her fiancé were also "cool" and did not require much. They basically let her mother plan the wedding while they lived together in another state. They have no complaints and think their wedding was perfect.

"I was in awe of my daughter during the wedding preparations," said one mother with tears in her eyes. She couldn't believe her daughter's style, proficiency, and good sense. She said that her belief that a parent provides the groundwork for a daughter to blossom was confirmed through working together on the wedding. It was definitely her daughter's wedding, and this mother felt great pride.

The Bride and Groom Prepare
for a Lifetime

One of the most important first steps a bride and groom can take while planning the wedding is to enroll in a marriage education course. Rapidly increasing in popularity, these courses aim to promote satisfying marriages. Their availability is listed on the Internet, and evaluations have shown that the courses help couples stay away from the pitfalls that can befall a marriage in its early years. One follow-up study of 150 couples who regularly attended a marriage mentoring program at Pacific University revealed that after five years not one of the couples had divorced.[7] A survey developed at the University of Minnesota is given to engaged couples and allows them time to sit and think about their compatibility. Known as the PREPARE survey, it deals with attitudes important to a solid relationship. A recent evaluation of the survey reported that 10 percent of those who filled it out ended up not getting married.[8] The goal of these courses, of course, is not to end engagements but to help ensure happy marriages.

Many churches require premarital counseling. A nationwide movement asks clergy to join together and agree to perform weddings only for couples who have undergone training in communication and conflict resolution. Clergy in cities around the country are cooperating. Even some civil weddings require marriage education—a growing trend as communities fight to prevent divorce and the subsequent effects on children.

One young couple talked about their prewedding course, required of the couples in their church. They opted for the half-day session rather than the longer course that took place over a weekend. The groom, who had attended reluctantly, enjoyed the course and said that a half day was enough for him. The bride also liked the course but noted that the most important, deep subjects, like communication, were not covered and could not be covered in one morning session. She felt the need for more in-depth conversation. Couples planning a wedding should be willing to devote a full weekend, or more, to talk about their future.

Most professionals in the field of marriage preparation believe that "marital satisfaction and success can be predicted on the basis of the quality of the premarital relationship and that marriages can be enhanced and stabilized through premarital interventions."[9] In other words, if a couple has major disagreements about how they live, work, or play together, marrying in order to improve the relationship doesn't work. A marriage course allows couples to become aware of those differences so they can seek help to resolve them before marriage. Or, realizing the chasms between them, they may choose to dissolve the relationship before they make a life commitment.

When marriage therapists were asked by researchers from Yale University to identify the problem areas in marriage, they rated the most significant problems as: lack of loving feelings, power struggles, communication, extramarital affairs, and unrealistic expectations.[10] The couples who could not resolve their differences during marriage counseling, according to the therapists, were unwilling to change or lacked commitment to their partner.

The selection of a marriage partner weighs heavily on a young person's mind and for good reason. The dread of having to change to satisfy a partner or the exhaustion from trying to improve chafes at both men and women. They want to be accepted and loved as they are, not become an image that a partner wants. When a young man who skied for a living described his very independent, accomplished architect girlfriend, I asked him if her strength interfered with their relationship. He responded "As long as she doesn't want to change me, we're okay." A sentiment both men and women share.

Young couples entering marriage, and especially those who

have gone together for a long time, have plenty of opportunities to test their compatibility and figure out if they have the problems that lead to marriage breakups. They should be realistic about their problem areas and not assume that marriage is a cure-all. *Before* marriage is the time for in-depth discussion.

"All You Get Is One Person"

In his autobiographical novel *TimeQuake*, Kurt Vonnegut writes: "Fifty percent or more of American marriages go bust because most of us no longer have extended families. When you marry somebody now, all you get is one person. I say that when couples fight, it isn't about money, sex or power. What they're really saying is, 'You're not enough people.' Sigmund Freud said he didn't know what women wanted. I know what women want. They want a lot of people to talk to."[11]

Vonnegut, in his flippant manner, taps into a deep need for emotional connections that engages both young women and women in midlife. Women satisfy that need with close women friends and with a spouse who becomes all persons: a mate who will listen, empathize, encourage, and share good and bad times. Perhaps Vonnegut wishes for the ancient days when a bride moved into the groom's neighborhood and became part of a large extended family. Then the man did not feel obligated to provide companionship for his wife (as Vonnegut seems to). His sisters and mother and cousins supplied friendship. But now many couples live far from their families and must depend on each other for emotional support. Their extended family consists of friends at home and at work, and they require nurturing to keep connected. The marriage relationship also requires nurturing.

Advice from a Bride and Groom

Julie and Bob met at a training program held by the computer company they had recently joined. Although they were in the same building, they didn't meet each other until halfway through the program when Bob and his friends threw a Super Bowl party for the trainees. When the training program ended, they found themselves at the same regional office, ensconced in cubicles next to each other. Julie used the word *clicked* to describe their first meeting, while Bob said, "We were so at ease with each other, and we had just met. I started looking forward to seeing her."

"One of the things I noticed about him," said Julie, "is that he is very perceptive about how people feel. When one of the women we worked with seemed to have a bad day, he would cheer her up." Bob was bringing to the workplace an attitude that young women are looking for. His personality helped make the office a cooperative, friendly place to work and Julie was attracted to that quality.

Because they worked so near each other, their romance flourished over the cubicle wall and was spurred on by their office friends. (They didn't comment on their superiors' reactions.) When Bob was transferred to a different office in another state, they began a long-distance romance, spending weekends together. They were engaged eleven months after they started dating. This was quicker than they had planned, but it was precipitated by Julie obtaining a job in Bob's city. Even though he was willing to have her move in with him, she did not want to. She had always said that she would not move in with anyone until she was engaged. It was not a pressure move on her part; that's what she valued. He knew he wanted to marry her at some point, even though he had hinted at five years down the line *if* they were still interested in each other. But her move made him decide to take the plunge.

Then the fun began. Although Bob was not nervous when he proposed because they had talked about marrying in the far distant future, he was afraid she would think he was joking and throw the ring into the water. (He proposed on the beach where they first had a long talk.) His nervousness, however, erupted during dinner after he had proposed. "At the end of the meal," he said, "my stomach was really upset, and I thought, Oh my God, what am I doing. It really hit me."

During the wedding preparations, Bob was startled to find he had to take a backseat. "Everyone on the male side told me to just let her plan everything, but that is not in my character. I had an opinion on everything." Julie and Bob therefore discussed most of the details and disagreed on only a few. For example, they couldn't agree on whether to have a trumpet or bagpipes at the wedding, so they settled on the traditional organ. Bob admitted that during the year of preparation, he was looking out for his mother's interests because he knew that she wanted certain things but wouldn't speak up (as a good mother of a groom).

The day went off "without a hitch," but they both acknowledged that their friends had a much better time than they did. When I asked if they had advice for other engaged couples, they willingly gave some bits of wisdom.

JULIE: Keep in mind it is not your day. You have your honeymoon. The wedding day is for your relatives and friends.

BOB: Don't serve seafood.

JULIE: Eat something during the day. We were married at 4 P.M., and I didn't eat anything all day.

BOB: Have an open bar.

JULIE: Be sure and enjoy your rehearsal dinner because then you're really relaxed.

BOB: Don't forget to dance with your mother-in-law.

JULIE: Remember the details are not what the wedding is

about. Whether you have blue dresses or pink dresses or an accordion player or a trumpet doesn't matter. The wedding goes by so fast that half the things you agonized over for hours are done in a split second. It really doesn't matter.

BOB: Check out the photographer. Whenever we would start to have fun, he would drag us away. He really hindered my enjoyment.

JULIE: Have fun tasting cakes.

BOB: Don't go wild on the food. People don't remember what they ate.

JULIE: Be sure and check the music. We had tapes of lots of bands.

BOB: Send cash, not gifts.

JULIE: Send gifts, not cash.

Julie and Bob were lucky in that their parents were happy with their choice of partner and, thankfully, have easygoing personalities. Julie and Bob also were not demanding and kept a budget in mind. Bob's family paid for the open bar. (He claims the bar bill "was like thirteen drinks per person"—not quite believable—even though drinks are often poured, abandoned, and poured again, abandoned again throughout the night.)

Both Julie and Bob said the best part of the wedding was seeing all their friends, from elementary school, high school, and college, gathered in one place. But they wished they had more time to spend with them that weekend. They envied their friends' free and easy time while they sweated out smiling for the photographer.

Although Julie and Bob's advice applies to their particular circumstances, their suggestions tap into some of the most sensitive times of a wedding and the overall enjoyment of the day.

Mother's Advice

Maureen has been the mother of two brides. Her older daughter, Cori, lived in another country but chose to be married in her hometown, where Maureen still lives. Maureen planned all the details of the wedding and consulted with Cori by phone and on her occasional visits. They had a great time and, she claims, no arguments, no second-guessing.

Her second daughter, Bobbie, also lived out of town but was married in neutral territory, a resort community where she had lived right after graduation. Since neither lived there and her daughter knew the area well, most of the preparations fell upon Bobbie.

Both her daughters were in their late twenties when they were married, had finally found careers that they liked, and were ready to settle down. Maureen loved her future sons-in-law. She was divorced but did not have the sole burden of the wedding expenses as her ex-husband was more than willing to pay for his daughters' weddings.

Because she had experienced the complete responsibility for one wedding and partial responsibility for the other, I asked Maureen to give some words of advice.

The most important thing mothers can do, she said, is to try their best to stay flexible and relax. When she mentioned the minor disagreements between her daughter and her, it struck me how inconsequential those matters were—like the type of basket for the flowers, the color of the tablecloths. Maureen also realized how absurd it was that two busy people (she worked full-time) could spend so much time on details. "When we disagreed," she said, "I didn't want to tell her that is the dumbest idea I've ever heard. Instead I would say, 'Let's figure this out together.' "

Maureen admitted that she told both her daughters, "I don't do well without tradition." So tradition formed the basis of both weddings. She and her daughters had "fun" planning the wedding, and one daughter sent her little "love notes" during the process. The only real objection she had was when Bobbie insisted that the color of the wedding cake had to be light green ("moss green"). In Maureen's mind, a wedding cake is white—not off-white or pale green, but white. The wedding cake was green.

Maureen proved flexible when she assumed all the duties for the first wedding and stepped back for her daughter at the second. If mothers and daughters could agree on as many things as Maureen and her daughters did (except the color of the cake), weddings would never create a blip in the mother-daughter relationship.

Most mothers are more concerned with the quality of the groom than the quality of the reception. Yet the groom's side of the wedding story seldom gets told. One brave groom has written a groom's tale.

Voices of Young Men

Kevin Ryan (his real name) decided that young men need a warning and sound advice before they venture into the wedding frenzy. His message is "Go to Las Vegas." His fanciful description of picking out floral arrangements for four hours, the agony of cutting the wedding list, the mayhem caused by ushers trying to fit into rented tuxes will convince brides (and their mothers) to be sympathetic to their grooms.

A groom is thrust into a woman's world and usually (always?) is at a loss. His usual defense is a quick retreat and a reappearance whenever his future mother-in-law has left town. Ryan, with tongue in cheek, warns young men about matters they should know before—and after—they walk down the aisle. Because *commitment* may be a hard word for a young man to get used to saying, Ryan defines it for them. "Commitment—As a bachelor you were taught to say that you were 'afraid' of it or you weren't 'ready' for it. But 'commitment' actually has no meaning whatsoever. Experts believe that the word originated with the Feminists in the 19th century, was actually defined once in 1955 and was finally abolished by the Women's Liberation movement in 1970. But when you're speaking to your girlfriend, be sure and mention commitment as if your life depended on it."[12]

Men, joking aside, want commitment as much as women. David Lipsky, the thirty-something author of *Late Bloomers*, writes: "Women tried wanting what men want; and then they went back to wanting what women want. And what women want from men is fine—the sex, of course, but also the person in the bed, in the airplane seat next to yours, across the tablecloth, riding in your head as you voyage through the day. Not many, just one. A witnessing presence. And the nice thing is, this is what men want, too. We know it is, because it is what everyone seeks out, and what they have always sought out. Men might complain about women, but the complaints seem intended mostly to establish a point about reluctance. You can learn this by spending an evening with a bunch of single men. They will talk about movies, about their jobs, or about their hobbies. But eventually, the conversation will wind itself around to the only point, and all they talk about is how much they want someone. For the sex, of course, but for the person in the bed, the woman in the airplane seat next to yours, the fellow passenger on your lifetime's voyage. That's what they want, too. The person who looks at you and says: you turned out okay. You are just the person I want to spend most of my time with. Somehow we spend all these months and years preparing a personality, piecing it together, testing it out on people, getting feedback from our pals. But the way you hand it in, the way you get it graded is when another person looks at you and says, You are just right. In all the world, you are the sole person I want to be with. Just you."[13]

That yearning for the "sole person" tells the age-old story of why men and women do find each other and do get married.

After the Wedding

The wedding is over. The bills are paid. The compliments are coming in, and once again, a mother must rethink her relationship with her daughter. The new husband is now her daughter's closest friend, soulmate, confidant. And the daughter must shift her focus, place her confidence in and build her connections through and with her husband. A new bride doesn't lose her independence; she gains an interdependence, a realization that she is never alone and will grow even stronger with her husband.

Mother and daughter now enter a new phase of friendship, one without an overlay of concern about marriage, about security. The mother now is a mother-in-law, a breed that is mocked by comedians and feared by new husbands. She knows through her own experience, and from comedians, that she must step aside and give the couple privacy. The best thing she can do for her daughter is to appreciate her son-in-law, refrain from making critical comments, and love him as a son. She will be amply rewarded with her daughter's gratitude.

Likewise, a bride must adapt to another mother, her husband's. Although this process may not be easy, one of the surest ways a young woman can endear herself to her mother-in-law is to never criticize her husband, at least not in front of his mother. His mother will love her because they both love her son.

As the excitement of the wedding and honeymoon fade into memory, the bond between a mother and daughter finds another depth as a mother sits back and appreciates her daughter in her many roles, which now include those of daughter-in-law, partner, spouse, wife.

12

Connected

T he voices of young women heard in these pages clearly speak of their desire for connections: connections to friends, boyfriends, coworkers, spirituality, families (including fathers, and especially mothers). They are women who do not want to stand alone in the world. But they also believe in developing themselves, the first step toward achieving true *inter*dependence—a relationship between equals.

No longer does a young woman succumb to the imperative that badgered women's lives twenty years ago, the psychological mandate to separate from their mothers. That dictate, demanded of boys as well as girls, set a course that destroyed the natural basic order and desire of human nature—to be part of a family. Families have always accepted (sometimes with difficulty) the oddball family members—the crazy uncle, the eccentric aunt, the curmudgeon grandfather. Daughters in this new generation don't turn away from mothers, even those who are difficult. They try to understand and empathize with their mothers. They are no longer driven by the belief that if they do not disengage from their mothers, they will lose their chance to be themselves. Young women feel free to form their own rules, to develop their own attitudes, to connect with whomever they wish. They freely connect with their mothers, some frequently, some infrequently, but they recognize the uniqueness and durability of the bond.

But not all is easy in their lives. Postponing of marriage has forced young women to mature on their own, and that delay of marriage brings with it a sense of uncertainty about the future. The angst many young women feel comes not from external pressures but from their internal drives. They know and appreciate what their families have given them and what society expects. They want to take advantage of opportunities, but figuring out priorities and how and when to act is not easily determined during their decade of the twenties. That is why connections mean so much. Connections offer the assurance that they are heading in the right direction. Girlfriends, boyfriends, and family are needed for support, advice, and solace.

The "we" generation may be more outwardly confident, yet they are more cautious than the generation of women who preceded them into the workforce of America. They are confident of their rights and their abilities, yet uncertain that they are making the right choices. They have seen the effects of divorce. They do not want to sacrifice family for career, as their immediate predecessors were inclined to do. Nor are they completely willing to sacrifice career for family. They want to find a middle ground, to pave new ways. How to find that way, when, at what age, contributes to their uncertainty.

These young women are acutely aware that they cannot control the outcomes of all life events. The epidemic of divorce and the shadow of AIDS challenged their certitude at an early age. Life, they learned, is not risk-free—even if they are not the risk-takers.

"I've grown up more than ever in the last five or six years," said a 26-year-old. "I don't know if it's because my parents got divorced or what, but I know when I was 18 I thought I knew everything. I look back on 18 now and think, Oh God, I knew nothing. I realize that I don't really know that much now, but I've learned a tremendous amount."

Many have learned a tremendous amount at a price—losing their sense of security. Offering their mothers comfort when they needed comfort themselves compelled some to postpone their own development. Now, in their twenties, they have caught up and regard their mothers as equals. They each have experienced anxiety and loss. The number of young women who have lost friends through disease or accidents astounds me. The reality of life in the fast pace of the United States has not evaded them. They have matured quickly and realize that life events can bring forth their inner strengths or create apprehension and withdrawal.

"What I think is interesting, based on the fact we are presented with so much opportunity, is that we are so much more aware than our parents, at least our mothers, of what we can do, what is expected of us. We're so much more attuned with what is perfect. We have to do the right thing, the best thing for ourselves. I think we strive and reach for our best potential, which I think is a great thing to try to reach for. But it is also a tough thing. It is a burden."

This 27-year-old states the dilemma well: She wants to reach for the best, but the best can be a burden. Can young women manage both reaching for the best and carrying the burden? These young women will applaud their friends who take on the challenge and will applaud their friends who choose to do otherwise. And that is the beauty of this generation. They accept each other's decisions, without judgment. They are familiar with indecision, with choices that turn out differently than expected, with disappointment. They share an uneasiness and trust each other. They seek each other's advice, company, and connection. They are truly the "we" generation. "We're pretty healthy women," commented another 27-year-old, and I agree with her.

The pride their mothers feel in their daughters is evident

throughout their conversations. I have been asked if I observed jealousy between mothers and daughters. That question doesn't even apply; it belongs to a different generation. These mothers are not envious of but rather enjoy their daughters' accomplishments. While mothers may at times regret that they did not have similar opportunities, they are thrilled that their daughters are using their talents, experiencing different cultures, meeting diverse people. Their concerns revolve around their daughters' love lives. Not because they want to interfere or feel the need to control, but because they want their daughters to make that important lifelong connection. They want to see them happily married.

The restlessness many mothers feel at midlife reflects their desire to reach out beyond family to develop their own selves. Their admiration of their daughters can spur them on to explore other options for themselves, in work, in friends, in community. They are inspired by their daughters, not jealous of them.

These mothers are role models for parenting, and their daughters freely acknowledge their gratitude. Because many mothers felt they could not satisfy their own mothers, they wanted a different relationship with their daughters. They have succeeded. Their daughters can talk about how much they love their mothers and how "incredible" their mothers are.

Both mothers and daughters realize the importance of family to their sense of self. They seek family cohesion, defined as "shared affection, support, helpfulness and caring among family members." Cohesion is not the same as enmeshment, which is psychological control and interferes with self-development.[1] These concepts often are substituted, one for the other, leading some to condemn family cohesion for putting a stranglehold on family members. Cohesion is just the opposite and leads to understanding and support—a quick telephone call to see if everything is all right, a sharing of experiences, an offer to help.

Will this quest for cohesion and sharing continue once daughters marry and have families of their own? Chances are they will marry. Mothers and daughters have endured through the difficult years of adolescent estrangement, agonized through the first years out of school and the first years without children, and formed a new closeness during the daughters' midtwenties and the mothers' midlife. The odds are that their relationship will continue to grow during the next phase of their lives.

Daughters who will be balancing marriage and work or marriage and work and children or marriage and children will not have the time to "chitchat" with their mothers as they may choose to do now. But if mothers remain as sensitive to their married daughters as they have been to their single daughters, their bond will grow even stronger in the next decade. They may have to search again for new connections between themselves and outside the family, but they have the stamina, goodwill, and motivation to succeed.

Perhaps the true test for each mother will come when she learns to step aside as her son-in-law becomes her daughter's closest connection. But stepping aside is not the same as stepping out of the picture. The mother-daughter bond is expandable and fully able to incorporate all aspects of the daughter's new life.

In each phase of their lives, mother and daughter will find new connections. A young woman and her midlife mother are just beginning their long friendship.

Notes

1. The Transition to Adulthood: The College Years

1. *IQ Issues Quarterly* 1, no. 4 (1996). Published by the National Council for Research on Women.
2. *Time* magazine, October 20, 1997, p. 37.
3. Charles J. Holahan, David P. Valentiner, and Rudolf H. Moos, "Parental Support, Coping Strategies, and Psychological Adjustment: An Integrative Model with Late Adolescents," *Journal of Youth and Adolescence* 24, no. 6 (1995).
4. Charles J. Holahan, David P. Valentiner, and Rudolf H. Moos, "Parental Support and Psychological Adjustment During the Transition to Young Adulthood in a College Sample," *Journal of Family Psychology* 8, no. 2 (1994), p. 219.
5. Alexandra G. Kaplan and Rona Klein, "Women's Self-Development in Late Adolescence," Stone Center, Wellesley College, Wellesley, Mass., 1985, p. 5.
6. Michelle D. Blain, Janny M. Thompson, Valerie E. Whiffen, "Attachment and Perceived Social Support in Late Adolescence," *Journal of Adolescent Research* 8, no. 2 (April 1993).
7. The commission was formed by Columbia University's Center on Addiction and Substance Abuse, and the report was issued June 1994.
8. Antonia Abbey, Lisa Thomson Ross, Donna McDuffie, and Pam McAuslan, "Alcohol and Dating Risk Factors for Sexual Assault Among College Women," *Psychology of Women Quarterly* 20 (1996).
9. Laurie L. Desiderato and Helen J. Crawford, "Risky Sexual Behavior in

College Students: Relationships Between Sexual Partners, Disclosure of Previous Risky Behavior, and Alcohol Use." *Journal of Youth and Adolescence* 24, no. 1 (1995).

10. "The American Freshman: National Norms for Fall 1997," Higher Education Research Institute, University of California, Los Angeles, December 1997.

11. Tracy R. G. Gladstone and Linda J. Koenig, "Sex Difference in Depression Across the High School to College Transition," *Journal of Youth and Adolescence* 23, no. 6 (1994).

12. Janet T. Spence and Eugene D. Hahn, "The Attitudes Toward Women Scale and Attitude Change in College Students," *Psychology of Women Quarterly* 21 (1997).

13. Constance Flanagan, John Schulenberg, and Andrew Fuligni, "Residential Setting and Parent-Adolescent Relationships During the College Years," *Journal of Youth and Adolescence* 22, no. 2 (1993).

2. The First Years Out

1. U.S. Department of Labor, Bureau of Women, 1996.

2. Bureau of Labor Statistics, reported in *Forbes* magazine, January 13, 1997.

3. "The American Freshman: National Norms for Fall 1996," Higher Education Research Institute, University of California, Los Angeles, December 1996.

4. "Uneasy Money," *Notre Dame* magazine 25, no. 4 (winter 1996–97).

5. Judith V. Jordan, "Relational Resilience," Stone Center Publication No. 57, Stone Center, Wellesley College, Wellesley, Mass., 1992, p. 5.

6. Ibid., p. 6.

3. Searching for Connections Through Friends

1. *The Random House Dictionary of the English Language,* s.v. "cooperation."

2. Deborah Tannen, *Talking from 9 to 5: How Women's and Men's Conversational Styles Affect Who Gets Heard, Who Gets Credit, and What Gets Done at Work* (William Morrow, 1994).

3. Jennifer Garbarino, John Gaa, Paul Swank, Robert McPherson, and Linda Gratch, "The Relation of Individuation and Psychosocial Development," *Journal of Family Psychology* 9, no. 3 (1995), p. 313.

4. Deborah Tannen, *Gender and Discourse* (Oxford University Press, 1994), p. 128.
5. Quoted in Carolyn G. Heilburn, *The Last Gift of Time: Life Beyond Sixty* (Dial Press, 1997).
6. Joan Borysenko, *A Woman's Book of Life: The Biology, Psychology, and the Spirituality of the Feminine Life Cycle* (Riverhead Books, 1996), p. 156.
7. Tannen, *Gender and Discourse*, p. 35.
8. Jan Yager, *Friendshifts: The Power of Friendship and How It Shapes Our Lives* (Annacroix Creek Books, 1997).

4. Communicating with Each Other

1. James C. Dobson, *Parenting Isn't for Cowards* (World Books, 1987).
2. Arlene G. Miller, "A Typology of Mother-Daughter Relationship Patterns for Young Adult Women and Their Mothers," *Issues in Mental Health Nursing* 16 (1995), pp. 377–94.
3. This research is noted in a study conducted by Linda Smith, Ronald Mullis, and E. Wayne Hill, "Identity Strivings with the Mother-Daughter Relationship," *Psychological Report* 76 (1995), pp. 495–503.
4. Ibid. p. 501.
5. Rosalind C. Barnett, Nazli Kibria, Grace K. Baruch, and Joseph H. Pleck, "Adult Daughter-Parent Relationships and Their Associations with Daughters' Subjective Well-Being and Psychological Distress," *Journal of Marriage and the Family* 53 (February 1991), p. 40.

5. Boyfriends

1. U.S. Bureau of the Census, 1996.
2. *New York Times,* May 11, 1997.
3. See, for example: Katie Roiphe, *Last Night in Paradise: Sex and Morals at the Century's End* (Little, Brown, 1997); Naomi Wolfe, *Promiscuities* (Random House, 1997); David Lipsky and Alexander Abrams, *Late Bloomers: Coming of Age in Today's America: The Right Place at the Wrong Time* (Times Books, 1994).
4. *Family Planning Perspectives* 26, no. 3 (May–June 1994).
5. Reported in *USA Today*, October 20, 1996.
6. *Family Planning Perspectives* 27, no. 1 (January–February 1995).
7. Ellen Fein and Sherrie Schneider, *The Rules: Time-Tested Secrets for Capturing the Heart of Mr. Right* (Time Warner, 1995).

8. U.S. Bureau of the Census, Population Division, March 1995 report.

9. K. Ames, "Domesticated Bliss," *Newsweek,* March 23, 1992, pp. 62–64.

10. Faith Monique Nicole and Cynthia Baldwin, "Cohabitation as a Developmental Stage: Implications for Mental Health Counseling," *Journal of Mental Health Counseling* 17, no. 4 (1995).

11. Elizabeth Thomson and Ugo Colella, "Cohabitation and Marital Stability: Quality or Commitment?" *Journal of Marriage and the Family* 54 (May 1992).

12. Nicole and Baldwin, "Cohabitation as a Developmental Stage."

13. Susan L. Brown and Alan Booth, "Cohabitation Versus Marriage: A Comparison of Relationship Quality," *Journal of Marriage and the Family* 58 (August 1996).

14. Renata Forste and Koray Tanfer, "Sexual Exclusivity Among Dating, Cohabiting, and Married Women," *Journal of Marriage and the Family* 58 (February 1996).

15. Stephen J. Bergman and Janet Surrey, "The Woman-Man Relationship: Impasses and Possibilities," Stone Center Publication No. 55, Stone Center, Wellesley College, Wellesley, Mass., 1992.

16. Ibid., pp. 8, 9.

6. The Midtwenties: The End of Option Paralysis

1. Gene Bocknek, *The Young Adult: Development After Adolescence* (Gardner Press, 1986), p. 81.

2. Erik Erikson, The Jefferson Lectures for the National Endowment for the Humanities, 1973. Quoted in *Mirabella,* May–June 1996, p. 77.

3. Jayne E. Stake and Linda L. Rogers, "Job and Home Attitudes of Undergraduate Women and Their Mothers' Sex Roles," 20, nos. 7, 8 (1989).

4. Phyllis Moen, Mary Ann Erickson, and Donna Dempster-McClain, "Their Mothers' Daughters? The Intergenerational Transmission of Gender Attitudes in a World of Changing Roles," *Journal of Marriage and the Family* 59 (May 1997).

5. Stephanie N. Mehta, "More Women Quit Lucrative Jobs to Start Businesses," *Wall Street Journal,* November 11, 1996.

6. Anne Fisher, "Readers Sound Off: Are GenXers Arrogant or Just Misunderstood?" *Fortune,* February 17, 1997, p. 139.

7. Quoted in the *New York Post,* March 11, 1997.

8. Linda Himelstein and Stephanie Anderson Forest, "Braking Through," *Businessweek,* February 17, 1997.

9. Joseph Stokes, Stephanie Riger, and Megan Sullivan, "Measuring Perceptions of Working Environment for Women in Corporate Settings," *Psychology of Women Quarterly* 19 (1995).

10. *New York Times,* November 10, 1996.

11. *Ms.* magazine, July–August 1996.

12. *Elle* magazine, December 1991.

7. Daughters of Divorce

1. Andrew J. Cherlin, *Marriage, Divorce, Remarriage* (Harvard University Press, 1992).

2. Ibid.

3. Arthur J. Norton and Louisa F. Miller, *Marriage, Divorce, and Remarriage in the 1990s* (U.S. Bureau of the Census, Department of Commerce, 1992).

4. Larry L. Bumpass and James A. Sweet, "National Estimates of Cohabitation," *Demography* (November 1989), pp. 615–25.

5. Frederick O. Lorenz, Ronald L. Simons, Rand D. Conger, Glen H. Elder, Jr., Christine Johnson, and Wei Chao, "Married and Recently Divorced Mothers' Stressful Events and Distress: Tracing Change Across Time," *Journal of Marriage and the Family* 59 (February 1997).

6. Judith Wallerstein and Sandra Blakeslee, *Second Chances: Men, Women, and Children: A Decade After Divorce* (Ticknor and Fields, 1989).

7. Ben Gore, "Study Finds Children of Divorced Parents Less Likely to Enroll at Selective Colleges," *Chronicle of Higher Education,* July 12, 1996.

8. Paul R. Amato, "Father-Child Relations, Mother-Child Relations, and Offspring Psychological Well-Being in Early Adulthood," *Journal of Marriage and the Family* 56 (November 1994).

9. Cherlin, *Marriage, Divorce, Remarriage.*

10. Paul R. Amato, "Explaining the Intergenerational Transmission of Divorce," *Journal of Marriage and the Family* 58 (August 1996), p. 628.

11. Wallerstein and Blakeslee, *Second Chances.*

12. Marion C. Willetts-Bloom and Steven L. Nock, "The Effects of Childhood Family Structure and Perceptions of Parents' Marital Happiness on Familial Aspirations," in *Divorce and the Next Generation: Effects on Young Adults' Patterns of Intimacy and Expectations of Marriage,* ed. Craig A. Everett (Haworth Press, 1992).

13. Joseph A. Marlar and Keith W. Jacobs, "Differences in the Marriage Role Expectations of College Students from Intact and Divorced Families," in *Divorce and the Next Generation,* ed. Everett.

14. Cherlin, *Marriage, Divorce, Remarriage.*
15. Nadine F. Marks, "Flying Solo at Midlife: Gender, Marital Status, and Psychological Well-Being," *Journal of Marriage and the Family* 58 (November 1996).

8. Three Generations: Daughters and Mothers Talk About Grandmothers

1. Wallerstein and Blakeslee, *Second Chances.*
2. Many of their stories are now being recorded. See, for example: Andrea Gabor, *Einstein's Wife: Work and Marriage in the Lives of Five Great Twentieth-Century Women* (Penguin, 1995); Jill Ker Conway, *Written by Herself: Autobiographies of American Women* (Vintage Books, 1992); Carolyn Heilbourn, *Writing a Woman's Life* (Norton, 1988).
3. Linda Thompson and Alexis J. Walker, "Mothers as Mediators of Intimacy Between Grandmothers and Their Young Adult Granddaughters," *Family Relations* (January 1987).
4. Maxine Kumin, "The Envelope," in *The Retrieval System* (Penguin, 1978).
5. Stephen R. Covey, *Seven Habits of Highly Effective People.* (Fireside Books, 1990), p. 235.
6. "1997 National Caregiving Survey," National Alliance for Caregiving and the American Association of Retired Persons, Bethesda, Md., June 1997.
7. Jeanne Walker, "When Parents Suffer Adult Children," *New York Times,* January 29, 1989.
8. Rosalind C. Barnett, "Adult Daughters and Their Mothers: Harmony or Hostility?" Center for Research on Women, Wellesley College, Wellesley, Mass., 1990.

9. Lesbian Daughters

1. Laura S. Brown, "Lesbian Identities, Concepts, and Issues," in *Lesbian, Gay, and Bisexual Identities over the Lifespan,* ed. Anthony R. D'Augelli and Charlotte J. Patterson (Oxford University Press, 1995), p. 4.
2. Ibid.
3. Quoted by Lawrence Van Gelder, *New York Times,* May, 1, 1997. The

name of this 1992 survey by the University of Chicago is the National Health and Social Life Survey.

4. Diana Baumrind, "Commentary on Sexual Orientation: Research and Social Policy Implications," *Developmental Psychology* 31, no. 1 (1995).

5. Michael S. Bailey, "Biological Perspectives on Sexual Orientation," and Celia Kitzinger, "Social Constructionism: Implications for Lesbian and Gay Psychology," in *Lesbian, Gay, and Bisexual Identities over the Lifespan*, ed. D'Augelli and Patterson.

6. Wendy B. Rosen, "On the Integration of Sexuality: Lesbians and Their Mothers," Stone Center, Wellesley College, Wellesley, Mass., 1992, p. 1.

7. Lennie Kleinberg, "Coming Home to Self, Going Home to Parents: Lesbian Identity Disclosure," Stone Center, Wellesley College, Wellesley, Mass., 1986.

8. Bryan Robinson, Lynda Walters, and Patsy Skeen, "Response of Parents to Learning That Their Child Is Homosexual and Concern over AIDS: A National Study," in *Homosexuality and the Family*, ed. Frederick W. Bozett (Harrinton Park Press, 1989).

9. Celia Kitzinger and Sue Wilkinson, "Transitions from Heterosexuality to Lesbianism: The Discursive Production of Lesbian Identities," *Developmental Psychology* 31, (1995). See also Laura S. Brown's chapter and Diana Baumrind's article in notes 1 and 4, above.

10. R. R. Troiden, *Gay and Lesbian Identity: A Sociological Analysis* (General Hall, 1988), quoted by Ronald Fox in *Lesbian, Gay, and Bisexual Identities over the Lifespan*, ed. D'Augelli and Patterson, p. 52.

11. Sarah F. Pearlman, "Heterosexual Mothers/Lesbian Daughters: Parallels and Similarities," *Journal of Feminist Family Therapy* 4, no. 2 (1992).

12. Robinson, Walters, and Skeen, "Response of Parents to Learning That Their Child Is Homosexual and Concern over AIDS."

13. Pearlman, "Heterosexual Mothers/Lesbian Daughters," p. 15

10. Searching for Spiritual Connections

1. Rebecca A. Clay, "Meditation Is Becoming More Mainstream," *Monitor* (September 1997), p. 12. Published by the American Psychological Association.

2. Kathleen Norris, *Dakota: A Spiritual Journey* (Houghton Mifflin, 1993), and *The Cloister Walk* (Riverhead Books, 1996).

3. Joan Borysenko, *A Woman's Book of Life: The Biology, Psychology, and Spirituality of the Feminine Life Cycle* (Riverhead Books, 1996).

4. Calmetta Coleman, "Seminar Tries Science to Revive Faith," *Wall Street Journal,* November 11, 1996.
5. Cheryl Heckler-Feltz, "Young Catholics Seek Sense of Belonging," *National Catholic Reporter,* August 15, 1997.
6. Susan Mitchell, *The Official Guide to American Attitudes* (New Strategist Publications, 1996). The General Social Survey is taken by the National Opinion Research Center of the University of Chicago and has surveyed American opinion since 1972.
7. Ibid.

11. The Wedding

1. Allan V. Horwitz, Helene Raskin White, and Sandra Howell-White, "Becoming Married and Mental Health: A Longitudinal Study of a Cohort of Young Adults," *Journal of Marriage and the Family* 58 (November 1996).
2. Linda Waite, University of Chicago, speaking to the Population Association of America. Quoted in the *New York Times,* April 19, 1995.
3. Scott J. South, "Sociodemographic Differentials in Mate Selection Preferences," *Journal of Marriage and Family* 53 (November 1991).
4. "The Joy of Being Single," *Businessweek,* September 15, 1997, p. 28. This article is based on research by David G. Blanchflower of Dartmouth College and Andrew J. Oswald of the University of Warwick.
5. Megan Fraser, "Wedding on the Web," *Greenwich Time,* September 19, 1996.
6. *Boomer Report,* October 1995, p. 2.
7. For descriptions of many of these courses, see Hara Estroff Marano, "Rescuing Marriages Before They Begin," *New York Times,* May 28, 1997.
8. The development of the PREPARE survey is discussed in Blaine J. Fowers and David H. Olson, "Four Types of Premarital Couples: An Empirical Typology Based on PREPARE," *Journal of Family Psychology* 6, no. 1, (1992). The 10 percent figure is quoted in the *New York Times,* May 28, 1997.
9. Fowers and Olson, "Four Types of Premarital Couples: An Empirical Typology Based on PREPARE," p. 10.
10. Mark A Whisman, Amy E. Dixon, and Benjamin Johnson, "Therapists' Perspectives of Couple Problems and Treatment Issues in Couple Therapy," *Journal of Family Psychology* 11, no. 3 (1997).
11. Kurt Vonnegut, *Timequake* (Putnam, 1997), p. 83.

12. Kevin P. Ryan, "Groom Tales," unpublished manuscript, 1997.

13. Lipsky and Abrams, *Late Bloomers,* p. 137.

12. Connected

1. Brian K. Barber and Cheryl Buehler, "Family Cohesion and Enmeshment: Different Constructs, Different Effects," *Journal of Marriage and the Family* 58 (May 1996), p. 433.

Index